JAPANESE CINEMA

DONALD RICHIE has long been the internationally acclaimed expert on the Japanese film. He is a former member of Uni-Japan Film and film critic for *The Japan Times,* and is presently Curator of the Film Department at the Museum of Modern Art, New York. He designed and presented the Kurosawa and Ozu retrospectives, as well as the massive 1970 retrospective at the museum, *The Japanese Film.* His book on *The Films of Akira Kurosawa* has been called a "virtual model for future studies in the field." Mr. Richie has been a resident of Japan for the past twenty-five years.

Film books by Donald Richie:

The Cinematographic View: A Study of the Film. 1958.

The Japanese Film: Art and Industry. 1959. Co-authored with Joseph L. Anderson.

Japanese Movies. 1961.

The Japanese Movie: An Illustrated History. 1965.

The Films of Akira Kurosawa. 1965.

George Stevens: An American Romantic. 1970.

Japanese Cinema

Film Style and National Character

Donald Richie

Anchor Books
1971
DOUBLEDAY & COMPANY, INC., GARDEN CITY, NEW YORK

This book is an extensively revised, expanded, and updated version of *Japanese Movies*, © 1961 by Japan Travel Bureau. Original material reprinted by permission of the Japan Travel Bureau, Inc., Japan.

Library of Congress Catalog Card Number 77-163122
Copyright © 1971 by Donald Richie
Copyright © 1961 by Japan Travel Bureau
All Rights Reserved
Printed in the United States of America

CONTENTS

LIST OF ILLUSTRATIONS

INTRODUCTION

THE JAPANESE FILM, WHICH WAS AMONG THE LAST TO achieve an individual flavor, is now the last to retain this individuality. It continues to show, for all who care to see, the most perfect reflection of a people in the history of world cinema.

This profile of Japan is easy to catch; the likeness is unmistakable, yet difficult to define. In the broadest of generalizations, it might be this: if the American film is strongest in action, and if the European is strongest in character, then the Japanese film is richest in mood or atmosphere, in presenting characters in their own surroundings.

The relationship between man and his surroundings is the continual theme of the Japanese film, one which quite accurately reflects the oneness with nature that is both the triumph and the escape of the Japanese people.

The Japanese regards his surroundings as an extension of himself, and it is this attitude that creates the atmosphere of the Japanese film at its best.

The content of the Japanese film is not much different from that of the film of other countries: motion pictures all over the world are concerned with the same things. Its period film is roughly equivalent to the American Western; its home drama is perfectly at home in England, France, or Germany. What is unique about the Japanese film is its form, the way in which the story is told, the angle from which it is viewed. This perspective accounts for the quality which we recognize as uniquely Japanese. We see it in the painting and the literature of the country, and we can recognize it in the language and in the lives of the people.

In the film we may begin by defining what it is not. One might think, for example, that in a country with some of the most developed theatrical techniques in the world, the influence of the traditional theater would be both natural and common. Yet this is not true. Noh has had no influence. Its use in a film like Kurosawa's *The Throne of Blood* (the witch, the background music, the timing of the intimate scenes, the makeup) was both conscious and experimental. Likewise, Kabuki has had small influence. Though some plays, notably *The Loyal Forty-seven Ronin,* are also screen favorites, the adaptations owe little to Kabuki style. When some elements do appear, as in Kinoshita's *The Ballad of the Narayama* or Shinoda's *The Scandalous Adventures of Buraikan,* it is a rare occurrence indeed. The influence of the Shimpa is seen in many of the themes of the Japanese film, but of its technique there are few traces; in fact, overcoming the influence of the Shimpa was one of the Japanese film's earliest triumphs. Even Shingeki, the modern theater (one quite analogous to that of America or Europe), has offered almost nothing to the Japanese film style. In the same way, television—a medium which has had an enormous and not always beneficial influence on the American film—has contributed as yet little to Japanese cinematic form. At most one might say (and it is, admittedly, saying much) that the influence of Japanese drama on Japanese film is interior. That is, the kind of mind which created the Noh and the Kabuki remains the mind which creates the Japanese film.

One might then think that the films of other countries have been a decisive influence, a common enough occurrence in France or America, countries which have eclectic cinematic traditions. And on one level there is some foreign influence. The Japanese "action" picture, particularly the gangster film, is much influenced by the American, as indeed are all the world's gang films. Yet on the higher level, as represented by the best directors, there is almost none at all. Or, perhaps better, there is none visible. In the history of each director there has been some. That we no longer see it in the most experienced directors leads us directly to a basic assumption in the definition of Japanese film style: the Japanese are unable to handle anything without sooner or later nationalizing it—or, perhaps better put, the peculiar Japanese genius is that of assimilation and incorporation. Any influence in Japan, be it gagaku or rock, is assimilated, digested, and turned into something sometimes rich, often strange, and always Japanese.

The process may take years, or it may take centuries, but the end result is a refinement, a distillation. Chinese ink and brush techniques have, in Japan, been rarefied into one of the most evocative, austere, economical, and aesthetically satisfying of art forms. Buddhist precepts have, as though under intense pressure, yielded *mono no aware*. The heightened form of the acceptance of the natural, which Japan shares with all of Asia, is also the result of the Japanese genius for assimilation. The art of the *bonsai*, the creation and cultivation of miniature trees; the natural artifice of Japanese landscape gardening; the open and visible structure of Japanese architecture—all speak of a truce with nature which the West has long found both mysterious and intriguing.

The equally Japanese tendency toward classification is another characteristic of the films. The Western director usually thinks of his film as an entity; the Japanese is usually conscious that he is working within a given genre. There is, as we shall see, the division between *gendai-geki* and *jidai-geki;* there are various subdivisions such as the *haha-mono* and *tsuma-mono*.

In all of the various genres, however, the treatment is somewhat dissimilar to that of the West, in that a film's initial assumption is not based upon a relative and philosophical good and evil but upon an absolute and social good and evil. One may affirm this, as does Ozu; may question it, as does Naruse; or may turn against it, as does Imai or Oshima. It remains a fact. Thus *Rashomon* with its multiple worlds of reality presented a line of thought uncommon to the Japanese.

In the Japanese drama there is usually but one reality; it is the rare drama or film that penetrates beneath the surface of existence. For this reason, perhaps, most Japanese films are more concerned with emotionalism than with any higher tragic feeling. To the Japanese, Hamlet is simply a faithful son avenging his father's death. He is consequently a good son, who loves his mother as all good sons should. One of the many reasons for this lack of what the Western world might consider the higher emotions is that the individual and his problems are—in art, if not in life—sacrificed to the well-being of society, and in Japan, society remains the family system.

It now becomes easier to appreciate the oblique perspectives of such directors as Ozu and Kurosawa. The former may affirm, and the latter may protest, but both statements are predicated upon a basic assumption involving the Japanese and the world he lives in. Ozu's strength as a film artist derives from the honesty of his affirmation, the beauty of his phrasing, and a flawless dedication to things as they are. Kurosawa's strength is the splendid vitality of his protest, the candor of his observations, and his superb technical facility.

This candor created the realism of the Japanese film style, one which, for better or for worse, has always insisted that life be seen as it is. This honesty created the films about ordinary people, about the lives of the unhappy, about life as it really is. And it reflects that feeling for nature, so utterly Japanese, which sees the natural world as an extension of man himself.

This attitude toward nature permeates Japanese art, the earliest poems as well as the latest films. It has developed the haiku, a poem in which the essence of a natural situation is fully suggested with an absolute minimum of words. In the haiku an occurrence or, more often, the conjunction of two occurrences is described, and from this conjunction a third image arises in the mind of the reader.

It is shown in the feeling for the elements: the rain scenes in so many Japanese films—Kurosawa's battle in the rain in *Seven Samurai;* the departure through the snow in Ichikawa's *The Outcast;* the almost palpable feeling of the sun in films as otherwise dissimilar as *Twenty-four Eyes* and *The Island.* Likewise this attitude toward nature is seen in the treatment of seasons: of which even the titles of Ozu's postwar films constitute a catalogue. *Late Spring* occurs just before the violence of the monsoon, a season of quiet and content and stillness. It is a parallel to the story, in which the daughter passes from the quiet content of unmarried life with her father into the stormier existence of a late marriage.

This Japanese love and understanding of nature is responsible too for the extraordinarily rich patina of the Japanese film. The Japanese is interested in how a thing is seen—indeed, often to the detriment of the thing seen itself—and he habitually sees it (in contradistinction to most other peoples) in its own natural context. The richness of *Ugetsu,* of *Rashomon,* of *Souls on the Road,* and of *Crossroads* is a consequence of the directors' realization that environment not only creates character but is also indispensable in communicating what this character means. The omniscient eye of *Seven Samurai* and *Ikiru;* the steady gaze of *Sansho the Bailiff* and *The Life of Oharu;* the calm regard of *Late Spring* and *Tokyo Story*—all are fundamentally concerned not only with seeing man and his environment but also with capturing that mood or atmosphere without the reality of which any view can be but partial.

The Japanese cinema at its finest has given the world a unique view of the human dilemma, and has interpreted this predicament with honesty and insight. By showing us man as an antagonist, with alternatives and the necessity of choice, it has given us a symbol meaningful to this century. It has given us the most perfect reflection of a people in the history of world cinema. More important, it has in the last analysis transcended the boundaries of race and nation, time and place, to produce an art form that moves us to an acknowledgment of our real selves, which—all considerations of culture and nationality aside—allows us partially to comprehend the pattern of life itself.

Elucidating this quality is what I have attempted in this book. For this reason one will find small emphasis placed upon the history of the Japanese film, and none at all upon its industrial basis. Those interested in a complete historical survey might read *The Japanese Film:*

Art and Industry, published in 1959, which I wrote with Joseph L. Anderson.

The present volume is based upon *Japanese Movies*, which was first published in 1961 by the Japan Travel Bureau and is now out of print. This is, at the same time, however, a new work. Not only does it include the past decade, its directors and their films, it also represents later thoughts and, hopefully, fresh insights. In addition, most of the stills used to illustrate the text are different from those in the earlier volume, and some are appearing for the first time in a Western publication.

The historical introductory sections are much the same, however, and it has again been most convenient to arrange the various directors in an admittedly somewhat artificial spectrum from right to left: that is, from those concerned with traditional values to those concerned with a more overt questioning of these values, or with other values entirely. If I have only briefly indicated the general loss of quality in the bulk of Japanese films—a hopefully transient state which first became obvious during the last decade—it is because I am concerning myself with an overall pattern and its continuance. If, in tracing the more elusive Japanese qualities of the Japanese cinema, I have perhaps seemed to suppress a number of films and a number of people important to Japanese film history, it is because I am tracing the development of a style and include consequently only those who most contributed to it.

Donald Richie
New York, 1971

1896–1945

In Japan the movies were popular from their first appearance, a Kinetoscope showing in 1896. Unlike in other countries, however, motion pictures were also considered respectable. In France the first films were just another distraction for the masses; in America they were patronized, thought of as bringing "plays . . . within the reach . . . of the poorest . . ." In Japan alone were they considered thoroughly respectable. An early Vitascope showing in 1897 was distinguished by a visit from the Crown Prince, later the Emperor Taisho. The early promoters added the glamour of the exclusive by asking, and getting, admission fully equivalent to that charged by the legitimate theater. By 1903, several years before England and America broke away from the store front nickelodeon, a permanent theater devoted entirely to films had been built in Tokyo. Thus, from the first in

Japan, the audience was composed of the relatively wealthy, those interested in the latest technical achievements, and that majority which—then as now—finds pleasure in contemplating the great wide world outside Japan.

When this early audience saw the waves at Deauville rolling toward them, or the locomotive arriving at the Gare du Nord, they were enjoying their first glimpse of the outside world, a thrilling experience to a people for centuries isolated from this world.

As might be expected, given the audience, the appeal of these early films was at least partially didactic: the audience went to be improved as well as entertained. Since Japan, like the rest of Asia, lacks almost entirely that antipathy toward being taught, which is often characteristic of the West, these early films, mostly those of the Lumière brothers, Louis and Auguste, and the Edison Company, found a ready and enthusiastic audience to whom learning what the French cavalry looked like, and how Fatima danced, were matters of the most lively interest.

This ready acceptance by an upper-class audience, however, had serious and complicated consequences, the most damaging of which was the equation of motion pictures with the legitimate theater. In America and England the audience did not go to the theater. They were not interested in the static, talky drama of the day. Thus the earliest films were about such action subjects as train robberies, the lives of firemen, and being rescued by Rover, subjects to which the motion picture is eminently suited.

The first Japanese pictures, however, contained not only 1904 street scenes and geisha dances but also the most celebrated stage actors of the day in action on the stage. In the West, the stage was still refusing to be compromised by the low-class novelty but in Japan the stage interested itself in the movies to the extent that at least several dramatic troupes commissioned early cameramen to film portions of their plays so that these could serve as advertisements at those theaters specializing in motion pictures.

Somewhat later the situation was to be reversed. In America the movies became socially acceptable only by the innovation of filmed theater with its "famous players"; in France by the stagy *film d'art*. In Japan the actors were to show less enthusiasm, realizing that movies are the natural enemy of the stage, and fearing that if they appeared in film no one would come to see them in the flesh.

Initially, however, the West was given time to develop at least the rudiments of film grammar and vocabulary before the stage took over; in Japan the influence of stage upon screen was from the first complete. Since no two art forms are further apart, the effect upon the infant Japanese cinema could have been disastrous.

The first Japanese films, as stagy as any *film d'art*, were burdened with all the accouterments of the Japanese stage. The continual front-center shot and the idea that actors must be seen full-length were limitations shared with other countries, but in Japan alone was there an insistence upon female impersonators and, the major obstacle to cinematic technique, the *benshi.*

The *benshi* was a narrator-commentator-explainer who accompanied most film showings until well into the era of sound, narrating a story which was at least occasionally of his own construction, commenting upon the apparent, and explaining the obvious. His popularity was extreme and was based upon that very quality which had made films so instantly popular: Japanese enthusiasm for self-improvement. Then as now the Japanese were unfailingly curious and, at the same time, unfailingly disturbed lest they not understand everything. This audience created the *benshi,* gave him his enormous prestige, and paid him his not inconsiderable rewards.

Although the *benshi* was not unique—America had its lantern-slide and travel-film commentators; France, its movie *compère*—he long outstayed his welcome and prevented the Japanese film from early attaining that reliance upon purely pictorial means which is the true strength of the motion picture. But he effectively filled a basic need, the need for complete instruction.

His effect upon the Japanese film is almost impossible to overestimate, and certain aspects of even the latest movies can be traced back to the *benshi* and to the need which he satisfied. Though Japanese films can be the most subtle in the world, the most understated, the most evocative, a commentator will frequently reiterate a point already presented visually. A scene will often appear, unnecessary in the context of the film, which explains what went before. Those Japanese critics who called *Rashomon* a profoundly un-Japanese film are, in a sense, correct. That ambiguity, that questioning of all absolutes which is the assumption of the Kurosawa film, is not one which is usually associated with the Japanese audience.

This early and total influence of the stage indicates the limitations which movies experienced in Japan. (In a sense the history of the Japanese cinema is the story of horizons widened and obstacles overcome.) For this influence was not long unchallenged, a fact which has made the Japanese film what it is today and explains why it in no way resembles the cinema of the rest of Asia: the stagy Filipino motion picture, the static Chinese film, or the infant cinema of Burma or Thailand where the local equivalent of the *benshi* is still in full power.

As early as 1909 a film by Shisetsu Iwafuji called *The Cuckoo* (Shin Hototogisu), a new version of an old stage favorite, tried to rely on visual images; it included the first Japanese flashback, just a year after D. W. Griffith in America had made his first important technical experiments.

The influence of the drama, it should be said, was not entirely negative. Though Noh and Kabuki have never influenced the cinema one way or the other, the contemporary theater—the Shingeki—indicated possible directions for the film, all of them different from those insisted upon by the Shimpa, an almost excessively theatrical form of drama which was designed to free the stage from the rigid conventions of the Kabuki, but which almost instantly fossilized into something even more doctrinaire. Shingeki at least concerned itself with a kind of reality.

An example was the 1914 film version of Tolstoy's *Resurrection*, a story which the Japanese have always found appealing and which had recently been seen on the Shingeki stage. It was called *Katusha* (Kachusha), was directed by Kiyomatsu Hosoyama, and—though stagy even by contemporary standards—it at least indicated a new direction and one which a growing number of Japanese filmmakers were insisting upon.

Among these were: Norimasu Kaeriyama, one of the first to attempt cinematic methods in the cinema; Thomas Kurihara, Frank Tokunaga, Yutaka Abe, and Henry Kotani, all of whom had worked in Hollywood; Kaoru Osanai, who introduced Konstantin Stanislavsky's acting method to Japan; and two directors of unusual talent, Eizo Tanaka and Minoru Murata.

Tanaka's *The Living Corpse* (Ikeru Shikabane, 1917), another Tolstoy adaptation, is perhaps typical of these early attempts to discover a suitable style. Female impersonators were used (in this case the heroine was played by Teinosuke Kinugasa, later director of *Gate of Hell*) and the acting techniques were still a bit broad for the intimacy of the screen. At the same time, however, Tanaka used natural settings whenever he could, tried to get his leads to act like people rather than actors, and—most important—attempted to tell his story in pictorial terms. The success was partial, for the early influence of the stage continued to be a handicap. In America, D. W. Griffith had indicated, two years before the Tanaka film, the precise nature of the American film style in the almost oracular *Birth of a Nation.* And in Denmark, Carl Dreyer was already at work on *Leaves from Satan's Book,* a picture which indicated a Scandinavian style we now see in the films of Alf Sjöberg and Ingmar Bergman.

Yet, if Japan stumbled into the film, it soon put a best foot forward. What these early filmmakers were able to accomplish in just a few years is seen in *Souls on the Road* (Rojo no Reikon, 1921), a picture in which Minoru Murata was assisted by Kaoru Osanai, and one which may be appreciated even today.

Other, and perhaps more representative films of the period, such as those of Shozo Makino, starring such popular favorites as Matsunosuke Onoe, are now as ludicrous as Sarah Bernhardt in *Queen Elizabeth,* so far different are the methods of the stage from those of the screen. But a picture like *Souls on the Road* remains emotionally compelling. Its story—two convicts who discover kindness, paralleled by the interlinked theme of the unwanted prodigal returning home—had some connection, however remote, with life as the audience knew it. Another reason is because Murata was interested in presenting a predominantly visual story in visual terms. Consequently one remembers the winter forest through which the convicts wander; the gray fields swallowing the errant son, his wife, and his daughter. While the story is as melodramatic as anything from the Shimpa, the fact that Murata refused to treat it as Shimpa makes the film memorable.

At the same time that a cinematic style was being

sought, the Japanese film began to interest itself in new subject matter. In France, Germaine Dulac was showing, in *The Smiling Madame Beudet*, that all marriages are not made in heaven, her film beginning where the conventional product ended; in Germany, G. W. Pabst was beginning to explore the lives of the underprivileged; in America, Henry King was looking at simple country life. Similarly, Japanese movies took an interest in subjects other than sword fights and pathetic tragedies taken from the stage.

Tanaka's *The Kyoya Collar Shop* (Kyoya Erimise, 1922) was one of the earliest films to treat realistically and sympathetically the lives of the lower classes. *Human Suffering* (Ningenku, 1923), directed by Kensaku Suzuki, was about the unemployed and women forced into prostitution, subjects which most producers, then as now, tended to avoid.

One of the most impressive of these films using new subject matter was the work of Kenji Mizoguchi, later to become world-famous as the creator of *Ugetsu*. The picture, *Foggy Harbor* (Kiri no Minato, 1923), was about a sailor, his girl, and her father, and was based at least partially on Eugene O'Neill's *Anna Christie*. What distinguished it, besides its subject matter, was Mizoguchi's formal framing of the story (it begins one evening and ends with the sunrise of the following morning); his insistence that a movie is meant to be seen; and his concern for the pictorial image which develops the story. He used very few dialogue subtitles and made everything so visually apparent that the services of the *benshi* would be rendered even more redundant than usual.

In other countries the search for cinematic style led to the achievement of a completely pictorial narrative. Only a year after the Mizoguchi film was released, F. W. Murnau made *The Last Laugh,* a picture almost without subtitles and one in which the images tell the entire story. In Japan, however, the use of titles was in itself an innovation and a blow for cinematic freedom, since they were aimed directly at rendering useless the *benshi,* an obstacle with which other national cinemas did not have to contend. Thus Japan never achieved the completely pictorial narrative because the arrival of sound, which finally did in the *benshi,* also rendered such a narrative unnecessary.

And, despite such experiments as those of Murata and Mizoguchi, the *benshi* was still very much in power. The audience, eager for instructive entertainment, flocked to hear him just as much as to see the picture. Though such films as *Souls on the Road* were constructing the cinematic vocabulary which would soon be taken for granted, the producing companies made little money on them. It is surprising that the directors were allowed to continue such unremunerative experimentation.

The reason they were was that times were changing. The female impersonators, though noisy in their dismay, were no longer used. Female stars, such as Sumiko Kurishima, became phenomenally popular. The 1923 earthquake completely shook up and consequently rearranged the industry, and foreign films were showing

Japanese audiences just how enlightening and entertaining motion pictures could be. *Intolerance* had been seen in 1919 but it was only after the earthquake, and the resultant shortage of Japanese films, that foreign pictures were imported in any number. Within a year such important films as *The Marriage Circle, The Covered Wagon,* and *The Birth of a Nation* had all been seen. The audiences now took much more readily to the experiments of Kaeriyama, Osanai, Murata, and Mizoguchi, which had helped form the basis of common Japanese cinematic style.

Like all true cinematic styles it was based upon realism, upon the fact that the camera cannot help but reflect reality, the style consisting in part of realizing and utilizing rather than attempting to disguise this fact. A film like *Souls on the Road* is just as realistic as, say, Henry King's *Tol'able David,* made in the same year, and is much more realistic than such stagy 1921 spectacles as Fritz Lang's *Destiny* or D. W. Griffith's atypical *Orphans of the Storm.* Realism, however, though it must be the basis of the style, is seldom more than that. The apparently actual must be made meaningful by both a selection and an interpretation. The way in which this has been done constitutes the aesthetic history of the film.

Some directors, like Griffith or Sergei Eisenstein, created the feeling of reality through cutting, through the structure, or the form of the film they were creating. Others, like E. A. Dupont and Dziga Vertov, called attention to the camera itself. Still others, such as Charles Chaplin in *A Woman of Paris,* Jacques Feyder in *Thérèse*

Raquin, Ernst Lubitsch, Erich von Stroheim, and G. W. Pabst, attempted to create entire worlds, with details so telling that the feeling of actuality became almost palpable. These directors presented characters along with the forces which motived them. Their eye for action was so acute that the result was psychological revelation.

The early films which helped form Japanese film style had an intimacy and a concern for detail which made them unusual. Murata and Mizoguchi were not merely telling stories. Rather, they were creating a world which faithfully reflected and sometimes illuminated the reality of Japanese life. Murata called his style "symbolic photographicism," by which he meant a kind of realism in which all the characters were lifelike but whose actions and personalities had symbolic and occasionally, as in *Souls on the Road,* almost allegorical meanings. Mizoguchi's aims were the same though his methods were different. Always interested in pictorial beauty, having studied to be a painter, he excelled in the creation of atmosphere, that almost palpable feeling of reality which is the special quality of the well-made film. Just as Murata wanted his characters to be real but also larger than life, so Mizoguchi, and those many more traditionally minded directors who followed him, wanted a world that was more realistic than life.

The creation of such a place is naturally one of the privileges of any film director. We approach the films of Von Stroheim, of Lubitsch, of Josef von Sternberg, of Max Ophuls, for example, as creations of the directors' own worlds, which obey their own inner laws and which achieve the feeling of something larger, more meaningful than raw life itself—which, in other words, results in art.

We are not, however, so familiar with a nation in which this impulse—and it is the aesthetic impulse—is so strong that the creation of such worlds results in a national style. When this occurs we are at a loss for words. We fall back upon "mood" or "atmosphere," or we talk about *mise-en-scène*. Few of these words come up in a discussion of, say, *Greed*, a picture made in the same year as *Foggy Harbor*. Yet they are just as applicable. Perhaps it is because "mood" has become a somewhat pejorative word; perhaps it is simply that we do not recognize it in our own films.

Atmosphere or mood is always the result of a sense of place. This is something which the Japanese themselves have to a degree uncommon in other countries. It is based upon that attitude toward one's surroundings—which may be called either "nature" or "reality"—which sees them as an extension of self. In the West the tradition has been man against nature: mountains are to be razed, rivers are to be dammed, the wilderness is to be opened up. It is difficult, therefore, for us to comprehend a culture that does not see man as powerful and immortal, at the center of the universe. The Japanese see him, rather, as part of the world he inhabits.

The celebrated Japanese concern for nature is a part of this. Traditional art shows mountains, sky, islands. A portrait is as apt to be that of a rock or a spray of bamboo as it is of a statesman or a merchant. Otherwise, the humans are small, appearing as tiny figures in boats or almost invisible on mountain paths. Traditional architecture carries nature into the house with the *tokonoma,* that alcove designed specifically for the hanging scroll and the flower arrangement. The traditional garden is designed to be seen from the house, just as the house is designed to be seen from the garden. The natural and the man-made thus enter into happy conjunction.

There is, even now in Japan, a welcoming of nature in most of its aspects (typhoons and earthquakes, equally a part, are not welcomed), which results in the mood of the Japanese house. In the same way there is in the Japanese film a willingness to see man as a part of all of nature, and this results in the atmosphere of the Japanese films.

Such an attitude is, of course, the opposite of a traditional Western idea, which implies that atmosphere is of little importance compared to character (the closeup) and action (the closely cut, plotted scene). These are important elements, and are by no means missing from the Japanese films, just as the Western film is often full of atmosphere. The attitude, however, is important. The traditional Western film does not linger nor does it seek such seemingly oblique ways of expressing emotion. Man remains very much the lord of his universe in movies from Europe and America. He never is in Japanese films.

One of the results is the common complaint that Japanese movies are too long, a charge aimed at the films of Yasujiro Ozu and the common sword-fight operettas alike. And it is true—either Japanese films are very long or else, since they do not move in the way we expect films to move, they seem long. Very well, we exclaim, we get the point, let's get on with it.

But to think that getting the point is the point of Japanese films is to miss the point entirely. Japanese art, traditionally, aims not at comprehension but at understanding. The Japanese themselves get the point fast enough, but they also feel that to comprehend something is not necessarily to understand it. To fully understand it is necessary to feel fully, and one's feelings, the Japanese believe, operate completely only after a certain amount of exposure. One needs time, in drama, in music, and in film, fully to immerse himself. To do so is to experience more deeply and this is one of the canons of Asiatic art.

There are a few analogies in Western cinema. Von Stroheim's films needed their orginal length—considered inordinate by traditional Western standards—because these pictures need their atmosphere. Abel Gance's three-panel *Napoléon* (made three years after the period we are discussing) needed, for the same reason, its original extreme length more than it needed its side screens. Michelangelo Antonioni's pictures must have every minute of their original running time. When you watch these long scenes with apparently nothing in them you either leave the theater or think about what you are seeing and begin to feel and consequently to understand the film the way the director intended. Antonioni had to force his audiences in the West, but in Japan he had an audience both willing and practiced. That Antonioni makes films much like a Japanese director is a comment still heard in Japan. Still, many in the United States find boring even the much-cut version of *L'Avventura*—which is all they have seen. Likewise, "beautiful but boring" is a comment one hears directed against Ozu's films, against even Mizoguchi's pictures. And it is indeed one of the singularities of the Western temperament that it will accept, even search out, the beautiful but will reject the boring. It will insist that beauty is in the eye of the beholder but that boredom is somehow imposed from without. Actually, to announce one's boredom is to announce one's own limitations.

The spectator is something like the camera lens. The less light there is, the more he must open himself up; and, conversely, the more he opens himself the more light he finds. And, in any event, there is nothing so fearful in being bored. It is probably preferable to being continually titillated because it leaves room for thought. Other peoples—those better able to live with their own limitations—even find it pleasant. To be boring, as the Noh play is undeniably boring, is merely another way of communicating. One enters the drama, or the movie, as one enters the rambling Japanese house or the twisting Japanese garden. It surrounds you; it is a world to inhabit.

The Japanese also find pleasant the overly familiar—one of our prime causes of boredom—and there is probably no land where the well-turned cliché is more admired. Most Western viewers, to be sure, are not aware of the clichés in an ordinary Japanese film until they begin to interfere with comprehension; until these viewers begin to complain that they cannot follow, say, the ordinary Japanese historical film. The reason is that the director assumes, rightly, that the Japanese audience already knows the story so well that he need not build what we would call convincing plot and comprehensive character. Sometimes this results in a further misunderstanding, as when Western critics found daring and Godard-like continuity-cuts in Inagaki's 1962 *Chushingura,* when all the director had been doing was skipping from one celebrated scene to the next. When the cliché is noted, however—the weeping mother, the invariably victorious swordsman—the same critics are quick to cry shame. Perhaps they are right to. At the same time, however, there are other cultures—most of those in Asia, all of those in the ancient world—where an apt use of cliché is to be admired. This is because clichés have a way of being accurate, and truisms always contain a truth. The Japanese film is thus under no constraint to avoid boredom, either indirectly through cliché and truism, or through length and inactivity.

One might more rightly complain about the truly excessive amount of sentimentality in Japanese cinema. From the earliest films right through Kurosawa's later pictures—the 1965 *Red Beard* (Akahige), the 1970 *Dodes'ka-den*—the complaint has been general, sparing neither the meanest mother-love picture nor the finest of Ozu's films. One must admit that if sentimentality is defined as a superfluous amount of emotion lavished upon an unworthy object, then the bulk of Japanese films are also sentimental.

One of the reasons is that despite or because of this feeling for nature, including human nature, Japanese society is so rigidly organized that it tends to discourage any of those larger objects of emotional concern. Hamlet's indecision, for example, is devoid of sentimentality simply by the size and importance of the object itself. Instead, the Japanese personal crisis is often of a nature, and a size, which the West would regard as inconsequential. To build an entire film around one of these crises and then to expect an outlay of emotion from both actors and audience strikes us as sentimental.

Given a deliberately limited emotional range, the Japanese can find few objects worthy of such emotional intensity. An exception is *Ikiru,* Kurosawa's 1952 film in which the emotional outlay is commensurate with the subject, a man's knowledge that he is dying. There are many more films, however, in which the same amount of emotion is expected of a long-suffering but otherwise healthy mother, a lovelorn but, in all other respects, contented young lady.

But then a charge of sentimentality (the Japanese, tellingly, have no word for this common emotion, they use the English) is not necessarily damning in Japan, nor is the word itself always used in a pejorative sense. When Kiyohiko Ushihara returned from a year's study with Chaplin in 1927, his consequent films *Love of Life* (Jinsei no Ai, 1927) and *He and Life* (Kare to Jinsei, 1928) earned him the title of "Sentimental Ushihara," but the adjective was considered more attractive than not. Until fairly recently "senchimentaru" was seen in advertising copy, intended to attract an audience. In the same way "merodrama" was an honorable description, and "tearjerker" (*namida chodai*) was a perfectly unexceptional way of speaking of those films which were somewhat laughingly classifed as one-, two-, or three-handerchief pictures.

While one cannot very well defend the emotional excesses of the ordinary Japanese picture, one must remember that there are many better films which are not. Furthermore, it was this ability to look deeply into the most minute of emotional states that, in part, resulted in one of the Japanese cinema's most important genres: the *shomin-geki*, films about lower middle class life as it is.

One of the qualities of *Souls on the Road* was that, for almost the first time, the lives of ordinary middle class people were shown. Due to the mildly fashionable beginnings of the cinema in Japan few indeed had been the appearances of the less well-off, unless they could be shown as picturesque farmer folk or the like. One of the results of the precedent of the Murata film was that, for the first time in Japan, directors were free to make films about the life of the average Japanese, unglamorized by the extremes of great wealth on one hand or great poverty on the other.

This had already occurred abroad once the influences of the *film d'art* were cast aside. Gustavo Serena's *Assunta Spinta* (1914) was about a working class girl; Jacques Feyder's *Crainquebille* (1922) was about the average poor; Jean Epstein's *Le Coeur fidèle* (1923) was about real, if criminal lower middle class folk. The Japanese *shomin-geki* was slightly different in that, from the first, it managed to avoid melodrama, that legacy from the stage, and strove for a balance between the sometimes humorous, sometimes bitter relations with a family, resulting in films about the economic struggle. This was the kind of picture many Japanese think of as being about "you and me."

The strength of this genre—later to become of prime importance, seen in its modern form in the films of Gosho, Naruse, Toyoda, and Ozu—was that, availing itself of the Japanese ability to create atmosphere, it could give its audience an emotional awareness of their own lives. Or, putting it the other way, the very real Japanese concern for showing things as they are resulted in an illumination of even the most trivial of human actions, returning to life much of the beauty and sorrow which living itself dulls.

The director who first—and some maintain best—realized this was Yasujiro Shimazu. He had been assistant director on *Souls on the Road,* was to become the teacher of Gosho, Toyoda, Yoshimura, Kinoshita, and began his *shomin-geki* career with *Father* (Chichi, 1924). This was the simple story of a sportsman and a country girl, and was intended as a comedy. Yet it relied so much more upon character and mood than on plot and slapstick that it became something more. In this film, in *Sunday* (Nichiyobi, 1924), and in *A Village Teacher* (Mura no Sensi, 1925), as well as in such later pictures as *Our Neighbor, Miss Yae* (Tonari no Yaechan, 1934), Shimazu evolved an extremely realistic, persuasive kind of film. He began by making sure that you laughed with and not at the characters. The films were entertaining but were also capable of making one feel. At the same time, one does not find the pictures sentimental because these lives are revealed to us as meaningful.

Though the West has no parallel for this kind of film or this kind of director, one thinks of the films of F. W. Murnau—particularly *Sunrise* and what is left of *City Girl.* In both pictures the director takes as his theme love among the lower classes and constructs a picture of such detail, such atmosphere, and works with such tact and concern that, despite the pathetic elements in both, we do not find them sentimental. This kind of skill, in avoiding the excesses of American melodrama on one hand, of Shimpa on the other, is not common in the West. That it became uncommonly plentiful in Japan is indicated by the extraordinary *shomin-geki* of Shimazu, Naruse, and Ozu.

One of the reasons for the surprising plenitude is that the Japanese, living closer to nature than most modern peoples, also, and consequently, live closer to their own natures. They are able to accept a kind of faithful and unflattering reality in the movies which the mass film audience in the West is only now beginning to tolerate. It is not that the Japanese are averse to seeing things as they wish them to be, as, indeed, hundreds of minor Japanese films have indicated. Rather, the Japanese, having a high opinion of reality, are literally much better able to appreciate a realistic rendering of their lives. Most peoples prefer to have their directors improve upon reality but the Japanese—though by no means averse to getting rid of life's little difficulties—are not afraid of being reminded

Souls on the Road, 1921. Directed by Minoru Murata. Mikio Hisamatsu, Denmei Suzuki, Haruko Sawamura.

The Kyoya Collar Shop, 1922. Directed by Eizo Tanaka. Arai Jun, Takeo Azuma, Hideo Fujino.

A Paper Doll's Whisper of Spring, 1926. Directed by Kenji Mizoguchi. Tokihiko Okada, Yoko Umemura.

A Tricky Girl, 1927. Directe
by Heinosuke Gosho. Emik
Yakumo, Atsushi Watanabe

Crossroads, 1928. Directe
by Teinosuke Kinugasa. Jun
nosuke Bando, Akiko Chi-
haya.

He and Life, 1928. Directe
by Kiyohiko Ushihara. Den
mei Suzuki (center), Kinuy
Tanaka.

Man-Slashing, Horse-Piercing Sword, 1930. Directed by Daisuke Ito. Ryunosuke Tsukikata, Jinichi Amano.

Life of an Office Worker, 1930. Directed by Yasujiro Ozu. Mitsuko Yoshikawa, Tatsuo Saito.

The Neighbor's Wife and Mine, 1931. Directed by Heinosuke Gosho. Satoko Date, Atsushi Watanabe, Tokuji Kobayashi.

Chorus of Tokyo, 1931. Directed by Yasujiro Ozu. Hideko Takamine, Emiko Yagumo, Hideo Sugawara, Tokihiko Okada.

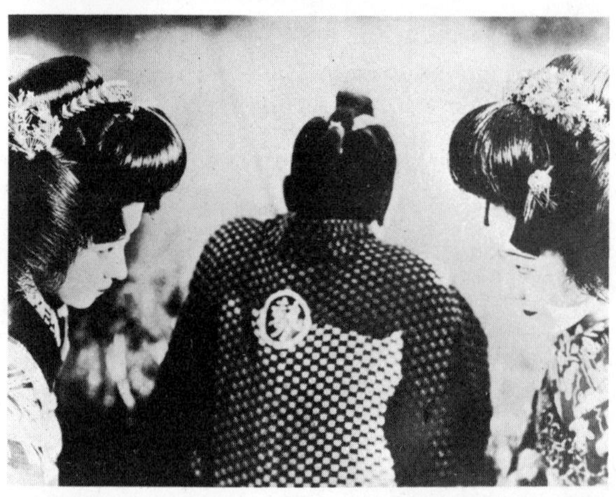

Peerless Patriot, 1932. Directed by Mansaku Itami. Junko Kinugasa, Isuzu Yamada.

I Was Born, But . . . , 1932. Directed by Yasujiro Ozu. Hideo Sugawara, Tokkankozo.

Taki no Shiraito, 1933. Directed by Kenji Mizoguchi. Tokihiko Okada, Takako Irie.

Our Neighbor, Miss Yae, 1934. Directed by Yasujiro Shimazu. Yumeko Aizome, Sanae Takasugi.

The Izu Dancer, 1935. Directed by Heinosuke Gosho. Kinuyo Tanaka, Den Ohinata.

Wife, Be Like a Rose, 1935. Directed by Mikio Naruse. Sachiko Chiba, Tomoko Ito.

Sisters of the Gion, 1935. Directed by Kenji Mizoguchi. Isuzu Yamada.

Osaka Elegy, 1936. Directed by Kenji Mizoguchi. Eitaro Shindo, Isuzu Yamada, Kensaku Hara.

Humanity and Paper Balloons, 1937. Directed by Sadao Yamanaka. Kanemon Nakamura (left), Chojuro Kawarazaki (center).

The Abe Clan, 1938. Directed by Hisatora Kumagai. Kanemon Nakamura (right).

Earth, 1939. Directed by Tomu Uchida. Isamu Kosugi, Bontaro Miyake.

Five Scouts, 1939. Directed by Tomotaka Tasaka. Isamu Kosugi (center).

Four Seasons of Children, 1939. Directed by Hiroshi Shimizu.

Mud and Soldiers, 1939. Directed by Tomotaka Tasaka. Isamu Kosugi (right).

The Story of Tank Commander Nishizumi, 1940. Directed by Kimisaburo Yoshimura. Ken Uehara.

Woman of Osaka, 1940. Directed by Kenji Mizoguchi. Kinuyo Tanaka, Yoko Umemura.

The Toda Brother and His Sisters, 1941. Directed by Yasujiro Ozu. Shin Saburi (left), Mieko Takamine (right).

Horses, 1941. Directed by Kajiro Yamamoto. Hideko Takamine.

There Was a Father, 1942. Directed by Yasujiro Ozu. Chishu Ryu, Haruhiko Tsuda.

South Wind, 1942. Directed by Kimisaburo Yoshimura. Shin Saburi, Chishu Ryu.

The War at Sea from Hawaii to Malaya, 1942. Directed by Kajiro Yamamoto.

The Blossoming. Port, 1943. Directed by Keisuke Kinoshita. Mitsuko Mita.

Sanshiro Sugata, 1943. Directed by Akira Kurosawa. Denjiro Okochi, Susumu Fujita.

The Life of Matsu the Untamed, 1943. Directed by Hiroshi Inagaki. Tsumasaburo Bando, Hiroyuki Nagato.

The Men Who Tread on the Tiger's Tail, 1945. Directed by Akira Kurosawa. Denjiro Okochi, Kenichi Enomoto.

An Enemy of the People, 1946. Directed by Tadashi Imai. Susumu Fujita (center).

of them on the screen. Just as the Japanese are unfailingly curious about the new, so are they unfailingly loyal to the old; just as they need to be constantly reassured about the unfamiliar, so are they consistently brave in the face of the all-too-familiar.

From this period on, more and more important directors turned, not to the improbabilities of the ordinary Japanese genres, but to Japanese life as they knew it: Mizoguchi's *A Paper Doll's Whisper of Spring* (Kaminingyo Haru no Sasayaki, 1926) about small businessmen in large cities, their difficulties, their sorrows; Hotei Nomura's *Collar Button* (Karabotan, 1926), about the trials of the white collar worker. Heinosuke Gosho, a pupil of and assistant to Shimazu—as were many of the directors later to determine the course of the Japanese film—came into prominence with *Lonely Roughneck* (Sabishii Rambomono, 1927), a great critical and popular success about the romance between a well-bred city girl and a rough but honest cart driver from the country. Later he made *The Neighbor's Wife and Mine* (Madamu to Nyobo, 1931), another simple story of the middle classes, which also happened to be Japan's first successful talkie. In it a husband cannot work because the lady next door, a very modern type, has a jazz band practicing in her house. This leads to a triangular situation, resolved when he is safely back with his wife. At the end, to the strains of "My Blue Heaven," the married couple take a walk through the suburbs in which they live, wheeling their baby carriage, both carried away by mutual memories. In the process they forget their little charge, left parked in the street in his carriage, and the final scene shows them scurrying back to duty, both romance and jealousy forgotten.

All of these films had in common a single subject: they were about the everyday lives of people just like those who came into the theaters to see the films; they were reflections, simple and honest, of ordinary people, about the sometimes humorous and sometimes hopeless relations within the family. The prevailing tone of these pictures became lighter as the directors grew more sure of themselves. The early films of Murata and Mizoguchi were serious films told in a serious manner. Those of Shimazu and Gosho, as well as those of directors such as Kiyohiko Ushihara and Yutaka Abe who specialized in the simple comedy, were serious films told in a lighter manner.

One of the finest, indeed one of the finest film comedies ever made, was Yasujiro Ozu's *I Was Born, But . . .* (Umarete wa Mita Keredo, 1932), a picture which contrasted the world of the adult with that of the child, which found the former lacking, yet at the same time recognized that innocence must have an end. The theme is the title: one is born . . . then the trouble begins.

A typical married Japanese salaried man—so typical that he might have stepped out of any *shomin-geki*—moves up the social ladder when he moves into the suburbs, near where his boss lives. His two young sons, however, do not adapt as well. They fight with the neighbor children, including the boss's son, and while attending an evening of home movies at the boss's house they suddenly see their father as adults see him, when he makes a fool of himself for the boss's camera. Angry, ashamed for him, they ask why he cannot be boss. He explains that that is not his position, that if he did not work, they would not eat. So the boys make the heroic decision to eat no more. The elder, voicing a truth apparent only to the innocent, says that he makes better grades and is stronger than the boss's son, that if he has to work for him when he grows up he might as well not even go to school any more. But the boys are only children. Their moment of truth over; seduced by empty stomachs, they forget and life goes on. They are not yet ready for the problem awaiting them.

That this sad, true, and moving film was also an extremely funny comedy is an indication of just how swiftly the Japanese cinema had matured. Films like this one and directors like Ozu are rare in any country, but seen in the context of history both are perfectly natural developments of a cinema that in only ten years had accomplished what others had taken thirty to create: the formation of a national cinematic style. It was a style based upon the ability of the camera to reflect perfectly things as they are.

This interest in the way things are accounts for much in Japanese life. The carpenter works with the natural grain of the wood, the stonecutter observes the natural form of his material; the gardener, the flower arranger, all begin with an observation of the nature of whatever they are working with. Films are about life, and it is not surprising that—sentimental excesses aside—little is done to violate life as we daily know it.

If we do not always recognize this, it is perhaps because the construction of the Japanese film is often different from that of the Western movie. We are sometimes unable to feel and hence to appreciate what the director intended. On the other hand, it is often this very construction (and *Ugetsu* is one of many examples) that allows a comprehension of life which Western cinema too often denies itself.

This was stated, accidentally and in reverse, by Sergei Eisenstein in his opinion that Japan is "a country that has in its culture an infinite number of cinematographic traits, strewn everywhere with the sole exception of—its cinema."

The truth of such a statement, however, depends upon one's definition of cinematographic traits. The Russian director found a vindication for his own editing methods in a misapprehension of the Japanese (and Chinese) *kanji* ideograph, and then wondered that Asian filmmakers did not follow his own mistaken assumptions. Actually, at the time, Japanese directors were developing their own style of editing, one which best suited them and what they were saying.

One of the problems lay, to be sure, in what the Japanese directors chose to say. Eisenstein once had the opportunity to see Gosho's early *Tricky Girl* (Karakuri Musume, 1927), a *shomin-geki* comedy, in which delight and pathos are beautifully combined. He disliked it, said that it began like a Monty Banks comedy but ended in deepest despair. What he objected to was its mixing of genres, of emotions, which most Westerners prefer to keep in separate compartments. Over and over the films of Ozu, of Naruse, of Toyoda—even of Kurosawa—have disconcerted the rigid West by successfully combining what are assumed to be antithetical.

The main problem—seen even now, after all the foreign directors between D. W. Griffith and Jean-Luc Godard have had their impact and made their mark—is that editing in Japanese films, which is a product of the Japanese mind, is reasoned but not rational. Because of this, Japanese films may appear illogical to the West.

That X follows Y, and is followed by Z, is a rational thought, an article of our intellectual faith. It is rational in that it is an act of ordering. But it is also only one of a number of possible modes of thought. Our law of cause and effect is logical and rational, but it does not invariably follow. It is not, in fact, a law. It is an assumption.

The mind itself does not, cannot, and need not reason in a continuous and connected manner. Reasoning is an invention of the eye and the ear, not of the brain. It was created the better to communicate, not the better to think. If one puts down thoughts in a single line and makes them interdependent, it is then simpler to indicate to someone else how the conclusion was reached, but this is after the fact of the thought itself. Thoughts come naturally in a scattered and illogical manner. Rational thought is itself a rationalization.

It is natural, since this is our sole mode of communicated thought, that all of our methods of such communication—novels, plays, films—should rest upon these assumptions: assumptions which are only now beginning to be questioned, in films as otherwise dissimilar as *Muriel* and *8½*.

There is, however, another way of ordering, one which is perhaps more illustrative of the actual workings of the mind. This is an ordering through association—a process we know mainly through *Last Year at Marienbad.* In Japan one sees it as early as *Souls on the Road,* where Murata edited associatively, doubling back and forth between his two stories, successfully striving to reinforce not ideas in opposition but emotions in parallel, cutting freely from one like state to another. One of the most spectacular examples of associative editing in Japanese cinema, however, remains Teinosuke Kinugasa's *Crossroads* (Jujiro, 1928).

The story is not exceptional. A young man believes that he has killed another man in a fight. Wounded, he goes to his sister for help. She, in turn, goes to an official to prevent her brother's being prosecuted. The official seduces her. She accidentally kills him. The brother then discovers that the man he thought he had killed is alive. Weak from loss of blood, he is killed by the shock.

Though unexceptional, not to say unpromising (even in 1928, samurai were expected to be heroic, not to run off to female siblings, and certainly not to die from the shock of *not* having killed someone) the story lent itself very well to Kinugasa's method of presentation. This was almost completely associative. Since the hero is no longer able to distinguish past from present, the film had no use for chronology and so dispensed with it. Rather, we see one image (the sister in her room concerned for her brother's safety) cut directly into another (his sister much younger, during their childhood), the link being neither logical nor causal but emotional. Later, the linkage becomes even more subjective. Pain becomes a visible hallucination when the water he is drinking turns to steam; the cat, attracted by his open, bloody wounds, becomes something evil, a black, creeping form. Again and again in this film the cut is determined not by its slight plot, not by the several convolutions of the story line, but because one scene suggests another or because one object suggests another: the round shape of a hat, the round shape of a teacup—an early example of what Eisenstein called analytical montage. The construction is largely made of such parallels and it is just in such a manner that many Japanese pictures are made, from the understated parallels of an Ozu picture to the hidden parallels in a Kurosawa film.

It is also indicative of Japanese film that though this picture was a period film—it was set late in the eighteenth century—Kinugasa treated it as though it were contemporary. That is, he put his audience into the mind of a living person, the hero of the picture. This is so rare in Western historical pictures that those who do so—Dreyer in *The Passion of Joan of Arc,* for example, completed a year before this film—are considered exceptional. In Japan this is not the only method of making a period film, but it is certainly a common one.

One of the reasons is that Japan is a young modern

nation with a very long feudal history. The country was opened to the West only a century ago, and this modern, democratic nation rests on a recent history, which is, to our way of thinking, medieval. A more important reason for this, however, is that the Japanese makes small distinction between the immediate and the long-past. He may now find Cary Grant an old-time actor but he would find Rudolph Valentino no more old-time. The present remains everything to the Japanese, which one might expect, given Buddhist doctrines on one hand and a lively sense of innate nature on the other. Consequently he is able to think of the past as though it were just last year. Also—and this is probably equally important—in the West we like to get something over with, label it and forget about it. The Asian too loves to label, but he is also forever taking whatever it is out of the box and fondling it again.

The result of this attitude toward the past is that it comes alive: far from simple pageantry it becomes something in which every member of the audience is actively involved. This immediacy is not only emotionally compelling; the degree of involvement assures the spectator's realizing that yesterday's problems are also today's. This not only brings the past near to the present in a way which Japanese usually find pleasing, it also suits the nature of film which, no matter how many flashbacks, is always in present-progressive tense; and it also offers filmmakers a tool by which the present may be evaluated—and criticized.

Unlike most Western peoples, the Japanese have a very

well-developed historical sense. Even now, despite the surface modernity of the country, the past continues to live. A part of the Japaneseness of the Japanese is this unquestioning and even casual acceptance of the past as a definite part of contemporary life. With this naturally goes some nostalgia, best seen in the ordinary period film which assumes that things were better back then, or, at least, were more interesting. At the same time, however, some directors had discovered that the problems of the present take on new dramatic contrast when cast in terms of the past. From this knowledge rose a very special and very Japanese film genre—and one for which there is no equivalent in the West: the serious period film in which history is presented with complete realism and the present is criticized in the context of the past.

Among those who developed this form—seen today in the films of Kurosawa, Kobayashi, Shinoda, and, occasionally, Imai—were Mizoguchi; Masahiro Makino, eldest son of the old-time director, Shozo Makino; Daisuke Ito, a pupil of Osanai; Hiroshi Inagaki; Mansaku Itami; and Sadao Yamanaka.

Ito's *Man-Slashing, Horse-Piercing Sword* (Zanjin Zamba Ken, 1930) is perhaps typical of these first period films which were oriented to the present. A young soldier is hunting for his father's murderer, an opening common enough to the average historical film. But, unlike those heroes, who always battle their way to the top, this one meets only reversals. Eventually, in order to live, he must steal from the farmers, who are quite as poor as he is. He learns that the reason for their poverty is the extreme oppression of the local government. He joins the farmers in their revolt, further motivated by finding that his father's killer is the local overlord.

In a film like this, made at a time of social unrest in Japan, the contemporary meaning is inescapable. One is reminded of the Russian films, then unknown in Japan. The near-symbolic soldier leading the common people is very close to certain aspects of, say, Vsevolod Pudovkin's *Storm Over Asia* (1928), the difference being that since Ito's hero was seen against a background of society, it was the resultant criticism of this all-too-established society which made the period film a vehicle for criticism.

Itami further enlarged upon the role of the period hero. His was never a hero in any conventional sense, but was, rather, a very ordinary man, weak in body if strong in spirit. Sometimes he was simply fortunate in doing the right thing at the right time, almost by accident. Itami's interest was not in showing costumed duels but in reflecting the social and political conditions of the Edo period, one which—for the director and for most of his audience—was a living and real part of contemporary Japan. *Peerless Patriot* (Kokushi Muso, 1932) was typical. It was about an impostor who took the place of the rightful master. The situation was developed in a satirical manner in which many of the feudal traditions, particularly those which survived in modern Japan, were ridiculed. That the impostor could in no way be told from the real lord resulted in a questioning of that basic feudal precept, the right of hereditary rule.

Other directors were not so much interested in social

criticism as in reanimating Japan's past in terms of the present. Hiroshi Inagaki, the only one of these early period directors still active, was interested in the past as key to the present. In a film as late, and as commercial, as *Musashi Miyamoto* (Miyamoto Musashi, 1954), shown abroad as *Samurai,* one can still feel the strength of the original concept: Musashi is not a mindless clotheshorse; he is a modern man.

The greatest of the directors who founded the exceptional period drama, however, was Sadao Yamanaka. He was not interested in social criticism but his objectives went far beyond historical reconstruction. His interest in the past was governed by a desire to show not merely its physical shape but also the emotions of which it was made. He attained his objectives through a heightened realism, of which his last film, *Humanity and Paper Balloons* (Ninjo Kamifusen, 1937), is perhaps the finest example.

The opening sequence is typical of the director. A former samurai has committed suicide. His friends talk about the death and one asks why he hanged himself like a merchant and did not disembowel himself like a true warrior. Where was his samurai spirit? The reply is that he no longer owned a sword, he had sold it to buy rice. This is the familiar death-theme opening, typical of the conventional period drama, but the difference in this film is enormous. In the conventional product the hero would have come to a glorious end, taking on twenty opposing swordsmen and only dying himself after having accounted for nineteen of them.

Though Yamanaka made only a handful of films, his influence has been great. Without him there would have been perhaps no *Ugetsu,* certainly no *Rashomon.* He was among the first—and, until after the Pacific War, the last—to see the past in terms of the present and to see it undistorted. He recognized the partial falsity of using the past to beat the present and, at the same time, scrupulously avoided the view of the common period film, which finds the Tokugawa age a romantic idyll for the juvenile mind. For him it was an era full of life and fuller of human problems. In this way, like Murata, Mizoguchi, Gosho, Shimazu, and Ozu, he took one more step toward a cinematic honesty, the attainment of which is the history of the Japanese film.

The past is, then, alive. This idea is not revolutionary in Japan, though it is elsewhere. In America, for example, beginning with *Stagecoach* and continuing through *Red River* and *High Noon,* the departures from Tom Mix and Hoot Gibson were considered so extreme that a new term—the "adult Western"—was found necessary.

Japanese cinema, on the other hand, offers a long and distinguished line of period films in which history is treated as contemporary. From Masahiro Makino's *The Street of Masterless Samurai* (Roningai, 1928), through the period films of Daisuke Ito, Hiroshi Inagaki, Mansaku Itami, Sadao Yamanaka, through Kurosawa's *Seven Samurai,* Kobayashi's *Harakiri,* Shinoda's *Assassination,* the finest period pictures have been those in which the past is presented with a concern for detail and a feeling for actuality, which most other countries reserve only for their films about contemporary life.

To be sure, Japanese cinema offers a variety of romantic sword-fight films about its feudal days, but the point is that the Japanese audience will also accept a realistic appraisal of the past. It is only in pictures such as Roberto Rossellini's *The Flowers of St. Francis* and *The Rise of Louis XIV*, such as Pier Paolo Pasolini's *The Gospel According to St. Matthew* and *Oedipus Rex*, such as Carl Dreyer's *The Passion of Joan of Arc*, and a few others, that the West has come to feel about the past as the Japanese have always felt.

One of the reasons is that in the West a part of the appeal of the past has been that it is, after all, passed—dead. It is summed up, decided upon. We accept the accomplished fact of this or that historical period and are rarely forced to consider that it too was once alive. Historical films, like historical novels, are always popular, and the reason is that they contrast the safely dead past with the possibly dangerous and certainly living present. We know what to think about what is gone—a person, an era; we never know what to think about what is still here. History is a closed book, we decide, and we know that we live in a wilderness of open-ended stories. Western historical entertainments therefore often purposely limit this endlessness, which is so disconcerting an aspect of living. Japan, however, is a country where a people are more willing to accept life as it happens to be, and there the attractions of an embalmed history, though present, are not extreme.

In any event there was, in Japan, an early public acceptance of the realistic historical film, an agreement from the man in the balcony that his problems were much like those of the samurai on the screen. Consequently, Japanese directors retained a freedom to make pertinent, living historical films, something which was often denied like-minded directors—and Dreyer is the most obvious example—in the West.

Not that the Japanese do not make historical distinctions. Indeed, in common use, the distinctions are indelible. The period film is always thought of as an isolated genre and it is indicative of Japan's attitude toward itself that it should make such a rigid division between the *jidai-geki*, the period drama, and the *gendai-geki*, the film about contemporary life. Yet this dichotomy exists only because of the traditional Japanese fondness for, and dependence upon, intellectual categorization. The continuum of history flows serenely over all barriers and the Japanese, in life as in films, quite accepts a living past. He no more questions this than he questions that, after a hard day's work, he comes home, takes off his business suit and gets comfortable in a kimono.

This, naturally, implies a double standard. There is no more truly logical connection between kimono and business suit than there is between the eighteenth and twentieth centuries. The Japanese is necessarily of two minds—mutually incompatible to Western eyes—about his world.

This pattern is reflected over and over in the Japanese film. It becomes a theme of the greatest importance to both the literature and the cinema of the country. It has, indeed, become the protean symbol of modern Japan: emotionally the present is a simple continuation of the past; at the same time the contrast between old and new is so glaring that it can lead to tragic complications.

One of the most perfect statements of this theme was Mizoguchi's *Sisters of the Gion* (Gion Shimai, 1935), a picture which has been called "the best Japanese prewar sound film." The sisters are geisha from Kyoto's well-known Gion district. The younger is quite modern, inclined to ignore the traditions of her profession in particular, Japanese traditional society in general; the elder possesses all the virtues of the legendary geisha. At the end the younger is in the hospital, the result of an automobile accident occasioned by her excesses; the elder remains too encumbered by tradition to rejoin the man she really loves, and of whom the younger disapproves. Completely conditioned by her code, the elder will always be afraid of going against custom; the younger, with every chance of recovery, will probably take up just where she left off.

If Mizoguchi's sentiments occasionally, and almost by default, went to the elder sister, his ending leaves her condemned. The problem suggested by the film, however, is a very vital one, and by implication goes far beyond the narrow world of the geisha. The situation is such that the spectator too must make a choice.

This problem of choice is one which animates all Japanese literature and, by implication at least, most Japanese films. In the Noh the choice has already been made before the play begins, and if the choice has been for personal indulgence over social or ethical duty one may be certain that ghostly or monstrous revenge is not far behind. In the Kabuki the choice constitutes the plot: will the lovers neglect duty because they love each other; can the hero bear to decapitate his own son, as duty plainly demands, so that his lord's son may be saved? Even lyric poetry reflects the choice: the elegiac quality of so much Japanese verse is occasioned by the poet's regrets—that he followed the path of personal inclination, or that he did not. This problem, a truly existential dilemma and one particularly pertinent to this century, is often brilliantly presented in the Japanese film.

Sometimes the problem becomes the theme, as in *Sisters of the Gion*. More often, however, directors are constitutionally on one side of the fence or the other. Indeed, one may categorize directors and their films by reference to their position regarding this most burning of questions. This is what I have done later in this book. Any generalization tends to be damaging but, in this case, the damage is slight. Any director worthy of the name in Japan continues to reflect, in no matter how oblique a manner, this most basic of Japanese facts of life. He may favor the traditional, as does Ozu, yet he is acutely aware of the disadvantages. He may fight against the traditional, as does Kurosawa, and yet any statement he makes is predicated upon its existence.

One of the results of the growing realism in the Japanese cinema of the thirties was a dissatisfaction with the traditional. The *shomin-geki* and the period film, if honest, could not show traditional life as being particularly pleasant. At the same time, then as now, polemic was rare; the dissatisfied found it enough merely to show things the way they were, this often amounting to condemnation.

An example is the late Tomu Uchida, a director since the twenties but whose best work did not appear until shortly before the war. *Earth* (Tsuchi, 1939), a near documentary, showed only what existed. It chronicled the seasons and used only the slightest of stories. A farmer loses his inheritance, is forced into poverty, is driven to despair, yet still manages to hope. It aimed at a complete naturalism yet was not so much interested in farm life, in the manner of a film like Georges Rouquier's *Farrébique,* as in the misery which life on the soil can entail, particularly in Asia. The interest in the seasons was not in their more decorative aspects, but as a manifestation of nature, a raw force, neither friend nor foe, against which farmers must traditionally struggle. The film was not unlike, and bears comparison with, Alexander Dovzhenko's 1930 picture of the same title; the difference is that while the Russian peasant landowners are struggling against the collectives, the Japanese are struggling against the very circumstances of their traditional heritage. Dovzhenko can show the triumph of the collectives; Uchida must show that peasants always fail but, at the same time, that they survive.

Another way in which dissatisfaction with the traditional was evidenced in Japanese films was in the number of pictures about children which appeared during the prewar years. A film such as *I Was Born, But . . .* which contrasts the world of the adult and the world of the child must necessarily find the former wanting, and it is just this adult world which represents tradition or things-as-they-are in films as otherwise dissimilar as Chaplin's *The Kid* and François Truffaut's *The Four Hundred Blows.*

Typical of these films was Tomotaka Tasaka's *A Pebble by the Wayside* (Robo no Ishi, 1938), a film so popular that it was remade in 1959. A little boy is apprenticed by a drunken father, though the child's teacher had wanted him to go to school. Later, after the mother's death, the boy is forced from one menial job to the next until he is rescued by the teacher. Throughout, the adult Japanese world was shown as uncomprehending at best. Everything was presented from the viewpoint of the child and, consequently, the sentimentality of the adult attitude toward children was missing.

This was certainly true of the films of Hiroshi Shimizu, whose *Children in the Wind* (Kaze no Naka no Kodomotachi, 1937) almost entirely ignored the world of adults. The later *Four Seasons of Children* (Kodomo no Shiki, 1939) was about some children who go to live with their grandparents after the death of their father. The child and adult worlds collide in scenes showing the over-indulgent and absolutely blind love for children which is so much a part of the traditionally Japanese attitude. Shimizu, while showing it, and even engaging in it himself, did not hesitate to criticize it, much of the power of the film deriving from the children's natural aversion to adult sentimentality.

The criticism was implicit. Shimizu was not interested in child psychology in the manner of Jean Benoît-Lévy, nor was he interested in making this world a microcosm of the adult world, as was Gerhardt Lamprecht in *Emil and the Detectives* (1932). He was interested only in the child's world, as seen by the child. If the result was an implied criticism of the traditional adult world, so much the better. This fruitful genre was not widely explored, however, and it was not seen again until well after the war, when Susumu Hani began making his first pictures.

The reason that such peaceful pursuits as films about children and further experiments in realism were suddenly cut short was that Japan was closing up for a state of protracted war. Pearl Harbor put an end to all such pursuits, but this did not mean the end of realism. Rather, it indicated a change of direction.

Realism as a style implies a somewhat passive attitude. The camera appears merely to record what life has to offer. Yet in even the most literal documentary, even in such films as those of Dziga Vertov or such seemingly casual documents as Luchino Visconti's *La Terra Trema,* casual in its construction if nothing else, selectivity is impossible to avoid. The common newsreel becomes just as much a portrait of its producer as *Potemkin* is, first and foremost, a portrait of Eisenstein.

In wartime Japan realism became a tool for propaganda and, as such, essential truths were twisted and turned, just as they were in other countries. Japanese film style, however, was not well suited to propaganda. The realism of the best Japanese films was and is compounded of a thousand small details, a seemingly prodigal but actually rigid selectivity, which creates on film an entire world, a whole atmosphere. An actor may lie during a scene shot in a studio set in which one does not believe anyway. But put the actor in natural surroundings, immerse him in a real atmosphere, show plainly the environmental forces which have made him what he is, and the lie will be palpable every time.

This is one of the reasons that the perversion of the realistic technique was not particularly widespread in Japanese wartime cinema. There were, to be sure, many propaganda and a few hate-the-enemy films; but at the same time there were pictures like Tomotaka Tasaka's *Five Scouts* (Gonin no Sekkohei, 1939), the first important Japanese war film and the one that established a pattern.

A company commander calls on five men; they are to reconnoiter and on their way are attacked. Only four return and, while his companions mourn, the fifth comes back. Soon the order comes to move out for general attack. This time they know there will be no returning. Death for some of them is certain.

To them war is not a reasoned endeavor. It is a thing—like an earthquake or a typhoon. One is caught up in it, becomes a part of it. The men run across open plains, not knowing where they are going. They burrow through cane groves, having no idea where they are. The enemy is like a fire, or a flood. One does not hate the destructive forces of nature; he only struggles against their power to destroy.

Other Japanese war films repeated this pattern again and again. These films were composed of the little things of which soldiers' lives are made: they are bored, they wait for mail; they search for flowers they knew at home. These films were essentially humanistic in outlook; they were made by those who opposed most of what the military stood for but were reluctant to go against what they considered unavoidable. Too, in a nation where obligation rather than feeling or reason rules the social order, it was not necessary to hide horror nor to present a rationale for war. It was necessary only to show the people what was required of them. Not that such films were actually any more common in Japan than they would be in any wartime country; still, the propaganda film was scarcely necessary. It was not even necessary for the militarists to inspire hate for the enemy: it was quite enough that the soldier was ordered to annihilate him. The soldier's feelings simply never entered into the question.

This, of course, is the traditional way at its most terrifying. But this is also the reason that some pictures which other countries would consider almost antimilitaristic were allowed to be made. Kimisaburo Yoshimura's *The Story of Tank Commander Nishizumi* (Nishizumi Senshacho-den, 1940) plainly reflected the prewar humanistic ideal. It showed its hero being friendly with enemy civilians, giving aid to a Chinese woman and her child, even fraternizing with his own men.

As the war progressed, however, the military proved less tolerant, demanding more from the directors. Kajiro Yamamoto, a pioneer in the new realism and whose *Horses* (Uma, 1941) was almost a documentary, was told to make *The War at Sea from Hawaii to Malaya* (Hawai-Marei Oki Kaisen, 1942) and did so with such realism that, despite miniature sets and studio shots, later Occupation authorities mistook some of the scenes for the real thing.

As pressures upon the directors became stronger, some made a strategic retreat into history, where they would be allowed a bit more freedom. Mizoguchi made films such as *Woman of Osaka* (Naniwa Onna, 1940), a very antitraditional picture in which members of a puppet-drama troupe (the Bunraku, who were just as traditionally conservative as is the Kabuki) were seen against Meiji-period Japan. Hiroshi Inagaki made *The Life of Matsu the Untamed* (Muho Matsu no Issho, 1943), a very cunningly constructed film in which it is never certain whether the hero's almost imbecilic adherence to traditional standards (he falls in love with a benefactor's wife; later, after the husband's death, he refuses to express himself, despite the fact that she now loves him as well, because it is not the proper thing to do) is a strength, leading to an eventual and glorious death; or whether it is pure weakness, making his life entirely worthless. At any rate, the ambiguity was such that in 1958 Inagaki remade the film into the very popular *Rikisha Man.*

Other directors pursued their own interests during

the war, insofar as they were allowed to, and in so doing furthered the Japanese film at a time when it might well have slipped back into the convenient staginess from which it had come. Ozu in *The Toda Brother and His Sisters* (Toda-ke no Kyodai, 1941) continued his development, uninfluenced by happenings around him. Akira Kurosawa came into public notice with *Sanshiro Sugata* (Sugata Sanshiro, 1943), a Meiji-period film which the government eventually decided to like because it thought it showed "the spirit of judo." Actually, it was also the first indication of the director's interest in the contemporary aspects of the past. Yoshimura managed to ignore the war in *South Wind* (Minami no Kaze, 1942), a picture about a man with good looks and no morals. Almost a light comedy, despite the seriousness of the times, it criticized society for its "money is everything" philosophy, taking a firmly civilian stand directly in the middle of the war. Keisuke Kinoshita's debut film, while apparently subscribing to an approved theme, actually turned it completely around. *The Blossoming Port* (Hana Saku Minato, 1943) was about two very sharp confidence men who deceive a small town into backing a fake shipbuilding company. The simple virtues of the islanders triumphed but in the process this genuinely funny, and innocently satirical film laid low not only the swindlers but also national policy.

Such pictures as these, however, were in the minority, particularly during the later years of the war. At the same time, the virtues of the Japanese film style were strong enough so that they could not be completely subverted. Realism might be used for propagandistic purposes but, at the same time, it remained the principal ingredient of the national film style. The concern for environment, for atmosphere, so much a part of Japanese cinema, though heavily criticized during the war for its "lack of optimism," remained a part of the film just as it has for centuries remained a part of the character. Though an unbiased view was directly opposed to the aims of the militarists, the Japanese ability to see the present in the past was by this time so strongly a part of Japanese motion picture style that even the most jingoistic of wartime period films were elevated by it.

All of these qualities managed to exist throughout the war and, in the years following, as though after a period of incubation, flowered in so luxurious a manner that foreign critics called it a cinematic renaissance. It was not that. Rather, it was the logical outcome of what had gone before. The golden age of the Japanese cinema had come.

1946–1971

JAPANESE TRADITIONAL CULTURE, SO PECULIAR TO THE country and so carefully handed down from generation to generation, remains so much a part of contemporary Japanese life that its appearance on film is not surprising. What is surprising is that so few directors interest themselves in its delineation.

This, of course, might be explained as merely the faithful reflection of contemporary Japanese life itself, that this tradition is now a much less strong force in the lives of the Japanese.

The tradition is the culture of beliefs and ways of thinking and ways of doing that has been preserved over many generations and which at last becomes representative. Japanese traditional culture, therefore, contains not only the geisha, but also the *chonan*, the eldest son and his multifold responsibilities; not only the tea ceremony but also arranged marriage; not only the Noh and the haiku but also the family system, that cornerstone upon which Japanese civilization rests.

Also, some distinction must be drawn between that traditional culture which remains a part of living Japan and that which is merely peripheral to it. In the movies the latter is represented by the *chambara*, the sword-fight film, and those heroes usually portrayed by such actors as Kinnosuke Nakamura and Kazuo Hasegawa. These are no more relevant to contemporary Japanese life than is the Robin Hood story to the English, or the acting of John Wayne to the American. Living Japanese tradition is seen mainly in the films of Yasujiro Ozu and Mikio Naruse, occasionally in those of Shiro Toyoda and —in a different way—in those of the late Kenji Mizoguchi.

The Japanese—film critic and paying customer alike—think Ozu the most Japanese of all directors. This does not mean that he is their favorite, though he has been given more official honors than any other; it means that he is regarded as a kind of spokesman. The man-on-the-street will tell you that "he has the real Japanese flavor."

This "Japanese flavor" has a much more definite meaning than, say, "the American way" or "the French touch" if only because Japan is so intensely conscious of its own "Japaneseness." Modern civilization is only one hundred years old and is a veneer over a civilization which has endured for two millennia.

This has created the familiar contrasts of the country, has given the Japanese his often near-schizoid intensity, and has made him extremely conscious of his differences.

These, after a certain time, he tends to guard. The career of many men of letters, and some not-so-lettered—politicians for example—show a similar pattern: a period of early exploration among things Western followed by a slow and gradual return to things purely Japanese. Over this another, more universal pattern is visible: when young, the Japanese is often more radically individualistic; older, he becomes more conservative, his very real individuality merges with the style of his people.

The career of Ozu followed these patterns, and in turn these patterns are celebrated in the Ozu film. Its tension is obtained by the confrontation of various individuals who are in different sections of the pattern: by confronting, for example, a father who has "returned" with a daughter who is on her "way out." And there is never any doubt on which side Ozu finds himself. It is for this reason that many of the young dislike his work, calling him old-fashioned and reactionary. And so he would appear, since he so continually celebrates those very qualities against which young Japan is constantly in revolt: the traditional virtues of Japan.

That these virtues are mainly theoretical in no way falsifies Ozu's position. Though everyday Japan is not a country noted for its restraint, simplicity, and near-Buddhist serenity, these qualities remain ideals, or virtues, and Ozu's insistence upon them and the public feeling for or against them make them more than empty hypotheses.

Take, for example, the quality of restraint. In a strictly technical sense, Ozu's later films are probably the most restrained ever made, the most limited, controlled, and restricted. He uses, for example, only one kind of shot. It is always a shot taken from the level of a person seated in traditional fashion on *tatami.* Whether indoors or out, the Ozu camera is always about three feet from floor level, and the camera never moves. There are no pan shots and, except in the rarest of instances, no dolly shots.

This traditional view is the view in repose, commanding a very limited field of vision but commanding it entirely. It is the attitude for watching, for listening; it is the position from which one sees the Noh, from which one partakes of the tea ceremony. It is the aesthetic passive attitude of the haiku master who sits in silence and with painful accuracy observes cause and effect, reaching essence through an extreme simplification. Inextricable from Buddhist precepts, its puts the world at a distance and leaves the spectator uninvolved, a recorder of impressions which he may register but which do not personally involve him.

Most Ozu films begin with a short sequence which illustrates this. The opening shots of *Late Spring* (Banshun, 1949) contain a scene inside a temple in Kamakura, the thirteenth-century capital of Japan and the beginning of what we now know as the Japanese way. Nothing happens. No one is visible. The shadows of the bamboo move against the *shoji;* the tea kettle is boiling, the steam escaping. It is a scene of utter calm. There is no subject, no theme, unless it is the gratefulness of silence and repose. This quality having been established, one of the characters enters and the story begins.

Empty rooms, uninhabited landscapes, objects (rocks, trees, tea kettles), textures (shadows on *shoji,* the grain of *tatami,* rain dripping) play a large part in Ozu's world, and the extreme simplicity of this view is matched by a like simplicity of construction once the film has begun.

Ozu also refrains from cinematic punctuation which other directors would think indispensable. As early as 1930 he had begun to give up optical devices commonly thought of as being necessary. He says that his silent *Life of an Office Worker* (Kaishain Seikatsu, 1930) was "a rare film for me—I used several dissolves. But this was the only time I ever did. I wanted to get the feeling of a morning beginning. The dissolve is a handy thing, but it is uninteresting. Of course, it all depends on how you use it. Most of the time it is cheating."

Several years later he was limiting himself even more severely. In *I Was Born, But . . .* "for the first time, I consciously gave up the use of the fade-in and fade-out. Generally dissolves and fades are not a part of cinematic grammar. They are only attributes of the camera."

This restriction, this extreme economy is further reflected in Ozu's manner of setting a scene, or indicating a setting. *A Hen in the Wind* (Kaze no Naka no Mendori, 1948) is set almost entirely in an industrial suburb. To indicate this, and to communicate the atmosphere, Ozu contents himself with a single image: a large gas tank seen from a distance; and, in conjunction, a river bank.

These two indications are all he needs and he returns from time to time to refresh our memories.

Often he will again and again use precisely the same camera setup to preface a sequence in series. In *Early Spring* (Soshun, 1956) scene after scene begins with early morning in the suburbs. Each of these morning scenes begins with a shot from outside the house: the morning express train in the distance, the neighbor's wife emptying her garbage. The same footage is not used but the shots are so similar that the effect is the same. Ozu wanted to capture the monotony of life in the city and admirably succeeded.

This concern for brevity and economy, this inclination for the ultimate in limitation, is naturally reflected in Ozu's choice of story material. Except for his early films (before he had achieved the eminence necessary to his insistence upon supervising the content of his pictures) his subject is always the same: it is the Japanese family.

His later films are about nothing else. In all of these the whole world exists in one family. The ends of the earth are no more distant than the outside of the house. The people are members of a family rather than members of a society, though the family may be unacknowledged, as in *Floating Weeds* (Ukigusa, 1959); may be a kind of family substitute, the small group in a large company, as in *Early Spring;* may be in disruption, as in *Tokyo Story* (Tokyo Monogatari, 1953) and *The End of Summer* (Kohaiyagawa-ke no Aki, 1961); or may be nearly extinct, as in *Late Spring, Tokyo Twilight* (Tokyo Boshoku, 1957), *Late Autumn* (Akibiyori, 1960), and (Ozu's fifty-third and final film) *An Autumn Afternoon* (Samma no Aji, 1962).

As a creator of the Japanese home drama at its best, he is much more interested in character and incidental incident than in action or plot, and has said: "Pictures with obvious plots bore me now. Naturally, a film must have some kind of structure, or else it is not a film, but I feel that a picture is not good if it has too much drama." Thus, in *Late Spring*, the interest is in the relations between a father and daughter; in *Late Autumn*, between a mother and daughter; and in both their varying reactions to the coming marriage of the younger. In *Tokyo Story*, Ozu examines the relations among three generations; in *Equinox Flower* (Higanbana, 1958), the effect of the gap between the generations. With little or no interest in plot movement, Ozu concerns himself with character development, and all of his better films represent a leisurely disclosure of character, the likes of which is rare in the films of any director.

Ozu's attitude toward films has always been that of a perfectionist, and in everything that he does in films the parts fit so perfectly that one is never conscious of the virtuosity with which it is done. His pictures are so subtle—in this sense, the precise opposite of Kurosawa's—that one never thinks to praise the skill with which his effects are achieved.

Some of Ozu's most memorable effects are those most apparently simple. In *Late Spring* there is a remarkable sequence where Setsuko Hara and Chishu Ryu, as daughter and father, watch a Noh performance. They do not move; neither does the camera. The sequence is intensely affecting, simply because of the carefully contrived context surrounding it.

In *Floating Weeds* there is a magnificent sequence—repeated literally from the silent *Story of Floating Weeds* (Ukigusa Monogatari, 1934)—where Ganjiro Nakamura has just discovered the machinations of Machiko Kyo. It is raining hard and they are on opposite sides of a narrow street, shouting at each other. The camera does not move but the characters, facing each other and accompanied by the incessant noise of the rain, range back and forth across the screen. The physical division of the street and the rain, their impotent fury, and Ozu's determination to let his camera (and himself) play no part, all conspire to create the power of this savage little sequence.

Ozu is at his finest when, after having prepared the context with a truly masterly care, he sits back, as it were, and simply watches. In *Equinox Flower* are two fine examples of the resulting vignettes. Kinuyo Tanaka, the wife, turns on the radio and we watch her delight as she listens to *naniwa bushi,* the old-fashioned music of her youth. Later in the film her husband, Shin Saburi, having made up with his errant daughter, is in the train on his way to see her. He looks aimlessly out of the window. Then he begins to hum to himself. In both of these tiny scenes we are so suddenly confronted with the delight of just being alive that the artful simplicity of these scenes results in a very real pleasure.

Perhaps Ozu's most typical effect is found in that most

typical film *Late Spring*. At the end of the picture the daughter, who has been living with her father, gets married. We know that she has finally gone only because the final scene shows the father alone. He is peeling a pear, and carefully turns the fruit round in his hands. His movements become slower and slower until he stops. The room is otherwise vacant, but this we are not shown. Rather, we see only his vacant glance, and thus we know. Then, not permitting himself even a sigh, the father begins again peeling the fruit and we know what will happen. After the picture ends, he will continue, his serenity contained.

The end effect of an Ozu film—and one of the reasons that he is thought of as a spokesman for the Japanese tradition—is a kind of resigned sadness, a calm and knowing serenity which persists despite the uncertainty of life and the things of this world. It implies that the world will go on and that mutability, change, the evanescence of all things, also yield their elegiac satisfactions. One lives with and not against time, as with environment. The Japanese call this quality (an essential manifestation of the Japanese aesthetic spirit) *mono no aware*, for which the nearest translation might be *lachrimae rerum*, Lucretius' reference to those tears caused by things as they are.

One usually sees the effect upon the father, though the other members of the family are certainly not immune. Still, Japan is a patriarchy—and Ozu always puts himself into his own films—and it is the father we remember longest, almost always played by Chishu Ryu, the perfect father image.

Critics have often pointed out that this final figure is actually Ozu himself. He delights in traditional Japan—as did Mizoguchi—and Ozu's fathers are usually connoisseurs of Japanese art: they collect old pottery or bronzes, they go to the Noh, they visit Kyoto.

Whatever value these observations may have, they do point to the origin of all the later Ozu films. They are much influenced by a literary form called the *shishosetsu*, the semi-autobiographical novel, and by the work of Naoya Shiga, a man specializing in this most popular of all Japanese literary forms. They are also influenced by and indebted to Kogo Noda, Ozu's long-standing collaborator, with whom he worked from almost the beginning of his career.

These films share with the *shishosetsu*, and particularly with the work of Shiga, what the critic Taihei Imamura has called "a Japanese attitude in that the observer tries to recall a phenomenon instead of analytically reconstructing it."

This Japaneseness of Ozu's approach, the emphasis upon effect rather than cause, emotion rather than intellect, is what—coupled with his ability to metamorphose Japanese aesthetics into terms and images visible on film—makes him the most Japanese of all directors.

He does not, however, have a monopoly on *mono no aware* nor upon traditionally Japanese themes and attitudes. His own personal attitude, if one compares the bulk of his films, was that the tradition he celebrated is dying, and that he regarded this as a tragedy. It is typical of Ozu's world that in it only the very young and the very inexperienced ever attempt to escape from the limitations of this traditional world. Ozu's successes are his fathers and the mothers in such films as *Floating Weeds* and *Late Autumn*, and their success lies precisely in their accepting these limitations as their own. As in that line from Robert Frost, they "find salvation in surrender."

The traditional Japanese view is limiting, for better or for worse. And the majority of Japanese film directors treating these values—and almost every Japanese director has, they are such a part of Japanese life—are agreed that the limitation is for the worse, though the dismissal is not always as abrupt as that of a Kurosawa or an Imai.

Both Mikio Naruse and Shiro Toyoda reflect traditional problems but are not content, as is Ozu, to reflect. They seem to imply that it is good that tradition dies or, at least, they show it as something from which their characters attempt to escape and cannot.

Naruse has said: "My films deal exclusively with the home. So do most Japanese films. It is in this fact that we find a major fault of Japanese pictures—the home is simply too narrow a place in which to set everything . . . Only if Japanese films can succeed in breaking beyond the limits of the family will they have truly universal meaning."

Thus, in a Naruse film, the family is usually held together by bonds so strong that no single member can break them. And, unlike in an Ozu film, they all want to, yet cannot. Life is a daily round of fixed customs and even the ways of expressing emotion are completely formalized. With all of the dramatic elements eliminated from the endless round of days and years, even the slightest personal emotional reaction has a major and usually unfortunate effect.

In *Mother* (Okasan, 1952), Naruse's "happiest" film, the mother, unable to support her family now that her husband is dead, has only the alternative of letting her youngest girl live with childless relatives, and the reactions of those few family members left almost tear the family apart.

That fine study of postwar despair *Floating Clouds* (Ukigumo, 1955) is a tragedy precisely because the young heroine, Hideko Takamine, decides that at least once she will get from life something that she wants. In *When a Woman Ascends the Stairs* (Onna ga Kaidan o Agaru Toki, 1960) the Ginza bar madame, again Hideko Takamine, is profoundly dissatisfied with her empty life. Yet when she makes one gesture toward freedom everything goes wrong. Cut off from all escape, she retreats into what she already knows, the very thing from which she was trying to escape. Again she climbs the stairs to her bar—the motif which appears again and again in the film with its wry and ironic suggestion of "getting to the top"—and in the final scene we watch her face change as she once more assumes the mask of entertainer, as she puts aside her feelings and takes up the art of pleasing. She greets her customers with the facile flattery her craft demands, she jokes, carries on as though nothing has happened. But we know that it has, that though we have seen only a small segment of her life, it remains the essence of her existence: nothing will change.

And nothing does in a Naruse film. The director once said: "From the earliest age, I have thought that the world we live in betrays us; this thought still remains with me . . . Among the people in my films, there is definitely something of [this] . . . if they move even a little they quickly hit the wall." And so they do, because in a Naruse film life is identified with the traditional Japanese life which he and most of his audience know so well.

Tragedy is constantly hanging over Naruse's characters and they are never more vulnerable than when they for once decide upon a personal, an individual, course of action. Yet tragedy need not necessarily be the conclusion. In the early *Wife, Be Like a Rose* (Tsuma Yo Bara no yo Ni, 1935), the daughter discovers that her estranged parents are able to find happiness in their unhappiness. In *Repast* (Meshi, 1951) the couple find that their differences, at least, make a bond. In *Evening Stream* (Yoru no Nagare, 1960) the young daughter, loving the lover of the mother, consciously turns toward the traditional life: she becomes a geisha. In *Bride, Wife, Mother* (Musume, Tsuma, Haha, 1960) there is an exquisite scene where the old unwanted mother gives in but does not give up. She has been to see a friend in the old peoples' home—a scene in which everything the two old ladies say has an irony of which they are completely unconscious—and later, waking at night and worrying about what to do, hears in the distance some drunks singing a song that the old people had sung. Then she sighs, merely sighs, and we know what she must do.

In *Untamed* (Arakure, 1957) Hideko Takamine—the perfect Naruse heroine—thinks of herself as completely free. Yet, at the end, in one of those long, quiet, resigned, final shots of which Naruse is so fond, we know there is little hope. Still, we know her well enough to know that she is going to go on trying, and that, somehow, is enough.

Even in the later films—*Yearning* (Midareru, 1963), *Scattered Clouds* (Midaregumo, 1967), and the others made before his death in 1969, where the control is less and a consequent sentimentality the more—Naruse remained true to his essentially tragic vision. At the extremely fine conclusion to his last great film, *Flowing* (Nagareru, 1956), only the elderly maid knows what will happen in the geisha house where she works, that the house is sold and they have only a few more days or weeks in which to enjoy a secure life. The others continue as they always have. The daughter, who will never again try to escape, happily works her sewing machine. The mother, filled with hopes for the future, practices her samisen. And in a long, unfolding final sequence, a kind of coda completely without dialogue, Naruse shows that their ignorance of approaching doom, their fortunate innocence, constitutes a kind of beauty, a kind of strength. Happiness is impossible but contentment, however unwisely based, may yet be achieved.

One of the reasons for the tragic bent of most Japanese

films, and the notorious predilection of the ordinary Japanese movie for the unhappy ending, is philosophical. Tragedy presumes a closed world, a contained place where values are known. Kabuki tragedy and Stuart tragedy can exist only where this premise exists—Tokugawa Japan, Cavalier England.

The Kabuki tragedy, for example, is usually based on the assumption that duty and inclination are incompatible. Yet, while it is tragic to believe that what one would like to do and what one ought to do are hopelessly far apart, it is at the same time reassuring because it so clearly defines one's choice. This seems especially comforting on the stage, or the screen, because this simplification can suggest that there is nothing more than this to life, that one now knows the worst. Hence the West clings to its *Hamlet* and Japan clutches at its *Forty-seven Ronin* because such tragic views do, at least, offer a kind of security.

Japan, which remains in many ways feudal enough to suggest a closed and finite world, prefers, perhaps more than other countries, tragedy to its apparent alternative, chaos. Yet it is just the fortuitous, the chaotic, the general meaninglessness of life, which the camera can and therefore must reflect. Cinema is at its most authentic when it is reflecting the apparently accidental, the seemingly unplanned. Both Flaherty's "slight narrative," and the open-ended stories preferred by some contemporary directors preserve a meaninglessness and, at the same time, impose a slight order.

The ending, for example. Neither the unhappy nor

the happy are honest. Only the open end is honest because life is open-ended. Life does not conclude, it merely stops, and this, in itself, implies continuity. This is the way of cinema because the movies are just like life. The very name of the early motion picture machine, the Vitascope, had—as Georges Sadoul points out—to do with "life."

Japanese film history shows us a people who in their cinema eventually realized this and turned further and further away from the all-or-nothing metaphysics of their classical stage. In the films of Ozu, of Naruse, of Mizoguchi, one finds an acceptance of the fortuitous, a "life is like that" smile which is as beautiful as it is useful. Such pictures are, of course, no monopoly of the Japanese —one remembers, from this same period, Alexander Dovzhenko's *Earth,* René Clair's *Sous les Toits de Paris,* Jean Vigo's *L'Atalante.* At the same time, however, such films were more common than in the West. What one regards as exceptional in Western cinema is a commonplace in Japan.

This accounts for the absence in Japanese film of both heroes and villains. One may find, to be sure, hundreds of Japanese pictures in which heroines are snow-white and villains are deepest-black but this, I submit, does not represent the true path of the Japanese cinema any more than such pictures in, say, America or Italy represent the true ways of those respective nations. Rather, in Japan as elsewhere, a recognition of the complication of human character is a prerequisite for any sort of meaningful experience, be it in life or on film.

The bias of Japan, however, insists that unattractive traits be accepted along with those perhaps more pleasing. There are many less reformed characters in Japanese cinema, and somehow becoming better is, indeed, not the major theme it has been in other national cinemas. Rather, bad is accepted along with good because it is there; it is part of things as they are.

This, of course, is again *mono no aware*, that awareness of the transience of all earthly things, the knowledge that it is, perhaps fortunately, impossible to do anything about it: that celebration of resignation in the face of things as they are.

Actions arising from this view of life are apt to be both melodramatic and sentimental but this is nothing against them, nor is the fact that some *mono no aware* films strongly suggest the Shimpa. After all, if a national theater can be said to reflect national attitudes and aspirations, Shimpa is a more representative national theater than, let us say, the Kabuki. *Mono no aware* films are sometimes unbearably sad and are often sentimental, but then, occasionally, so is Japan.

If Ozu actively celebrates the traditional life and Naruse actively dislikes it, we have at least two clear statements on the subject. Other directors, even those most concerned with it, seem, by comparison, irresolute. But from this irresolution comes a pliability which is perhaps more representative than anything else of the authentic Japanese attitude.

Shiro Toyoda's view of traditional culture is decidedly ambivalent and yet, perhaps because of this, most of his better films find him involved with it. The young heroine of *Wild Geese* (Gan, 1953), a film known abroad as *The Mistress,* falls in love with a student she never has an opportunity to meet again. In the manner of all Naruse heroines she is punished for daring individuality. Then, in a long and extremely beautiful final scene, she wanders over the meadows where she first spoke with the student; turning, she watches the wild geese fly from the marsh. Toyoda turns to catch her face—and finds hope. We know all we need to complete the story.

In *Snow Country* (Yukiguni, 1957) the young geisha is traditional at heart and completely unaware of it. She considers herself very modern and part of this modernity is the kidding relationship she maintains with a young artist. Toyoda deftly removes the mask in one fine scene toward the middle of the film. The artist asks her to find him a geisha. Since she herself is a geisha, what he means—and his manner of asking makes it clear—is that he wants someone to sleep with. Until now their relationship has been that of geisha and casual customer, a relationship devoid of meaning and almost asexual in its playfulness. He has now, however, let her know that he is interested in more. Her reaction, wonderfully controlled both by Toyoda and by Keiko Kishi, playing the role, is one of confusion and retreat. She attempts to resume the traditional role of the geisha, artificial laughter, simulated disbelief, childish petulance. And, so far had she formerly discarded this role with him, she fails. Eventually she must lose her temper in order to retain her traditional self-respect. This brilliant piece of character analysis is followed without comment by a master stroke: the very next scene, late at night, finds her drunk, coming into his room and flinging herself at him.

In their separate ways both the geisha and the young heroine of *Wild Geese* overcome tradition and Toyoda's occasional animosity toward the traditionally Japanese is, unlike that of Naruse, only rarely stated. One of his fullest statements, however, is found in one of his finest films: *Grass Whistle* (Mugibue, 1955).

It is the story of three adolescents, the girl still a child, the boys just growing into that long and difficult period which is prelude to manhood. They are good children, if a bit wild, and—like all children—they manage to live entirely outside the traditional society represented by their parents. But they are not immune to it. Their tragedy is not merely the coming of adulthood and the consequent loss of the candor of childhood, more specifically it is their subscribing to attitudes and beliefs, properly traditional in themselves, which have no relevance to their own problems.

One of the boys dies. His friend had loved him, and the girl had loved him; and, in the honest manner of children, both boy and girl also love each other. In the final sequence of the film they go to the grave of their friend and the boy attempts to tell her what he feels. Already old enough to distrust her emotions, she almost hysterically subscribes to whatever ideas of morality she has already absorbed from the grown-ups. It becomes evil to think of herself in the presence of the dead—rather, she must remain faithful to a memory which is already false. And in the final scene—a snow storm on the beach where only the summer before the three had been children together—she runs away from the boy who loves her and whom she loves, leaving him to face alone this first indication of the quality of being adult.

Toyoda's perhaps typical ambivalence is seen in films like the uneven *Evening Calm* (Yunagi, 1957). The heroine—Ayako Wakao, then Japan's most modern modern-girl—discovers that her mother is a prostitute and the boy she herself is in love with is her own half-brother. This admittedly disconcerting turn of events turns her against her completely untraditional mother. In the final scene we find her in kimono, working in a bookstore, and very properly refusing to assist a foreigner who is looking for books on the Yoshiwara, the old licensed quarter of Tokyo. Toyoda has said that he finds her actions "beautiful," and that "she acts as she does in order to protest the ugly confusion of present-day Japan." In other words, in order to protest she turns toward the traditional.

Perhaps because he, like so many Japanese, directors or not, has decidedly ambivalent feelings toward the traditional patterns of Japanese life, Toyoda's best films are those in which he treats an essentially serious theme—the conflict between the demands of a traditional society and the always untraditional inclination of the individual—in a comic manner.

In that delightful comedy *A Cat, Shozo, and Two Women* (Neko to Shozo to Futari no Onna, 1956), Toyoda has the dense but individualistic hero, beautifully played by Hisaya Morishige, much more in love with his cat than with either of his wives. This brings him into direct conflict with both his mother and the first wife, absolute dragons of respectability. And also, oddly, with his second—a mambo-crazed modern type. Shozo's position is that of so many Japanese: he is equally repelled by both extremes. He resents tradition but is afraid of the anarchy of complete personal freedom. Shozo is only happy with his cat, an animal absolutely selfish but reassuringly domesticated.

Marital Relations (Meoto Zenzai, 1955)—probably Toyoda's finest film—takes the same theme, the compromise between traditional ideals and personal freedom. This is a story of a charming young no-good and his somewhat unwilling geisha mistress—played by Hisaya Morishige and Chikage Awashima—who eventually and almost uncomprehendingly give up every one of the benefits of the traditional Japanese life—respectability, power, material well-being—in order to be together. But the true strength of this very funny and very sad film is Toyoda's tacit assumption that, since both are selfish, they are really thinking of their own personal freedom. Yet, unable to make the final break, which would be from each other, they—like lovers in some comic inferno—are doomed to each other's loving companionship throughout life. This is emphasized in a bittersweet coda (somewhat resembling that lovely final scene in *A Cat, Shozo, and Two Women* where the hero, drenched by a summer shower, finally finds his cat and, picking it up, says: "We will go away together . . . we won't come back,") where the wastrel and the fallen geisha go off in the snow together, a scene all the more clever in that it is a completely recognizable parody of the *michiyuki,* that Kabuki convention where the traditional lovers set out into the cold, cold world.

In Japan as elsewhere comedy makes the unpalatable not only sweet but nourishing and though Toyoda has used the same theme over and over again—notably in the serious but excellent *Twilight Story* (Bokuto Kidan, 1960)—he has not again equaled the humanity of *Marital Relations,* a film which perfectly epitomizes the dilemma of the Japanese caught between mutually contradictory values—an epitome, perfectly recognized by the Japanese audience, which made it one of their most popular films.

And it is an awareness of humanity, its aspirations and its longings, that sets the traditionalism of Toyoda or Naruse off from that of Ozu and Mizoguchi. The message of the latters' films—if works of art so perfectly self-contained can be said to have a message—is that freedom is found in limitations. The message, much more apparent, in the films of Naruse and Toyoda, is that the price of freedom is high. It means complete loss of all security (something which the Japanese perhaps more than most people fear). Only the very strong—Naruse's characters are admittedly weak—can possibly afford it.

Hence, perhaps, the attitude of these latter directors toward the young. Toyoda openly champions them. "I think that, even though humanity is filled with ugliness,

No Regrets for Our Youth, 1946. Directed by Akira Kurosawa. Setsuko Hara, Susumu Fujita.

Utamaro and His Five Women, 1946. Directed by Kenji Mizoguchi. Toshiko Mizuka, Minosuke Bando.

The Record of a Tenement Gentleman, 1947. Directed by Yasujiro Ozu. Choko Iida, Reikichi Kawamura.

Drunken Angel, 1948. Directed by Akira Kurosawa. Takashi Shimura (right).

Late Spring, 1949. Directed by Yasujiro Ozu. Setsuko Hara, Chishu Ryu.

Stray Dog, 1949. Directed by Akira Kurosawa. Takashi Shimura, Toshiro Mifune

A Picture of Madame Yuki, 1950. Directed by Kenji Mizoguchi. Michiyo Kogure, Eijiro Yanagi.

Until the Day We Meet Again, 1950. Directed by Tadashi Imai. Eiji Okada, Yoshiko Kuga.

Rashomon, 1950, Directed by Akira Kurosawa. Machiko Kyo, Toshiro Mifune.

Carmen Comes Home, 1951. Directed by Keisuke Kinoshita. Hideko Takamine, Toshiko Kobayashi.

Clothes of Deception, 1951. Directed by Kimisaburo Yoshimura. Machiko Kyo, Ichiro Sugai.

Repast, 1951. Directed by Mikio Naruse. Setsuko Hara, Ken Uehara.

A Tale of Genji, 1952. Directed by Kimisaburo Yoshimura. Mitsuko Mori, Kazuo Hasegawa.

The Life of Oharu, 1952. Directed by Kenji Mizoguchi. Kinuyo Tanaka.

Ikiru, 1952. Directed by Akira Kurosawa. Yunosuke Ito, Takashi Shimura.

Mother, 1952. Directed by Mikio Naruse. Chieko Nakakita, Kyoko Kagawa.

Children of the Atom Bomb, 1953. Directed by Kento Shindo. Nobuko Otowa.

Tokyo Story, 1953. Directed by Yasujiro Ozu. Chieko Higashiyama, Setsuko Hara.

Ugetsu, 1953. Directed by Kenji Mizoguchi. Masayuki Mori, Machiko Kyo.

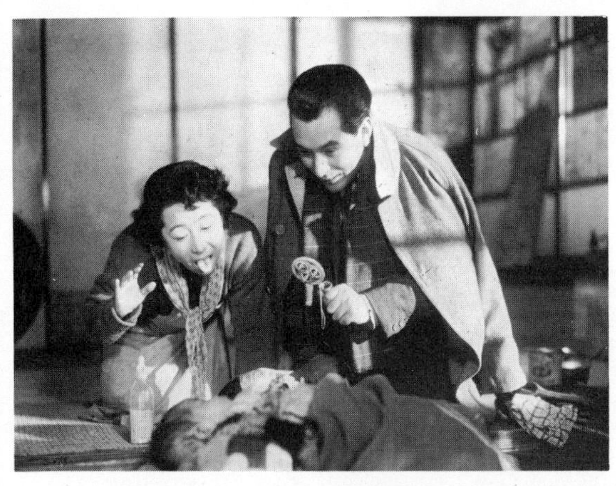

Where Chimneys Are Seen, 1953. Directed by Heinosuke Gosho. Kinuyo Tanaka, Ken Uehara.

The Thick-Walled Room, 1953. Directed by Masaki Kobayashi. Shinji Nambara.

A Japanese Tragedy, 1953. Directed by Keisuke Kinoshita.

Wild Geese, 1953. Directed by Shiro Toyoda. Hiroshi Akutagawa, Hideko Takamine.

Muddy Waters, 1953. Directed by Tadashi Imai. Yoshiko Kuga.

An Inn at Osaka, 1954. Directed by Heinosuke Gosho. Nobuko Otowa (center), Shuji Sano (right).

A Story from Chikamatsu, 1954. Directed by Kenji Mizoguchi. Kyoko Kagawa, Kazuo Hasegawa.

Sansho the Bailiff, 1954. Directed by Kenji Mizoguchi. Kinuyo Tanaka (left), Chieko Naniwa (second from right).

Seven Samurai, 1954. Directed by Akira Kurosawa. Seiji Miyaguchi (left).

Sounds from the Mountain, 1954. Directed by Mikio Naruse. So Yamamura, Setsuko Hara.

Twenty-four Eyes, 1954. Directed by Keisuke Kinoshita. Hideko Takamine (center).

Marital Relations, 1955. Directed by Shiro Toyoda. Hisaya Morishige, Chikage Awashima.

Growing Up, 1955. Directed by Heinosuke Gosho. Hibari Misora, Somegoro Ichikawa.

The Beauty and the Dragon, 1955. Directed by Kimisaburo Yoshimura. Nobuko Otowa (center).

Floating Clouds, 1955. D
rected by Mikio Narus
Masayuki Mori, Hidek
Takamine.

*She Was Like a Wi
Chrysanthemum,* 1955. D
rected by Keisuke Kin
shita. Noriko Arita, Shin
Tanaka.

Grass Whistle, 1955. D
rected by Shiro Toyod
Kyoko Aoyama, Akira Kub

beauty still exists, particularly in the younger generation. This is perhaps the reason that I am so interested in it."

One finds in the films of Naruse and Toyoda a very sympathetic attitude toward the young. The heroines of *Wild Geese* and *Floating Clouds* break with traditional virtue and the directors approve. The second wife in *A Cat, Shozo, and Two Women* is shown as dreadful but she is certainly no worse than the hidebound first. The younger brother's wife in Naruse's *Anzukko* (1958) is perhaps a rather extreme example of the untraditional girl—she makes her husband do the laundry—but she is not unsympathetic.

On the other hand, Ozu's young people are treated in a very hard manner indeed. The errant daughter in *Tokyo Twilight* is killed; the office flirt in *Early Spring* is ostracized. The young people in *Floating Weeds* and *Equinox Flower*, even the children in *Good Morning* (Ohayo, 1959), a partial remake of *I Was Born, But . . .* are saved only by their forced inclusion into the family unit. Ozu differs markedly from a director like Heinosuke Gosho, who shows people escaping from the traditional and approves them, as in *Where Chimneys Are Seen* (Entotsu o Mieru Basho, 1953); or thoroughly disapproves the traditional, as in *Growing Up* (Takekurabe, 1955); or who romanticizes it, as in *Firefly Light* (Hotarubi, 1958). Ozu would seem to believe the traditional even beneficial. If he, instead of Gosho, had made *Growing Up*, one wonders if he could have brought himself to approve of enforced prostitution. To be thoroughly consistent he should have found the ideal restraint in the girl's assuming one of the greatest burdens which a traditional life—and not only Japanese—can bring. But then Ozu has never stressed the stultifying and even ugly aspect of the traditional in Japan, with its helpless stifling of what is most original in human beings. For certain directors, and I would guess for a majority of the Japanese people, the terrors of the traditional life are balanced by its attractions.

This is certainly true of the films of Noboru Nakamura, a director upon whom it is popularly if wrongly assumed that the mantle of Ozu descended, after the latter's death in 1963. In films such as the very long *The Ki River* (Ki no Kawa, 1966) and *The Three Faces of Love* (Sekishun, 1967) traditional Japan is celebrated and denigrated to an equal degree. Missing entirely is Ozu's complete acceptance. Concerned with the extremes of emotion, Nakamura neglects the undramatic middle position where, in Japan as elsewhere, true wisdom lives. Ozu's ethical achievement is that he shows us this in a manner which makes its truth inescapable. By eschewing plot he revives story; by his rigorous manner of viewing he gives us new vision; by showing rather than telling he allows us to apprehend the transcendent. In comparison, Nakamura's view of the traditional is commonplace. Beauty become prettiness and tragedy becomes pathos.

A fairly recent example of the attraction of the traditional is afforded by Keisuke Kinoshita. His films describe almost perfectly that pattern of return mentioned earlier, the period of early exploration, usually among things

Western, followed by a definite homecoming to things Japanese.

Kinoshita made fun of the traditional, particularly the family system, in such films as *Broken Drum* (Yabure Daiko, 1949), in which the title refers to the paper tiger of a father; *Carmen Comes Home* (Karumen Kokyo ni Kaeru, 1951); *Carmen's True Love* (Karumen Junjosu, 1952); and the savage little satire *A Candle in the Wind* (Fuzen no Tomoshibi, 1957). Later, however, Kinoshita began interesting himself in a defense of just that which he had been attacking.

To be sure, the change was not sudden. The quite effective, and affecting, *Twenty-four Eyes* (Nijushi no Hitomi, 1954) had presented the traditional life—that of a school teacher, Hideko Takamine, her tribulations, her joys—in a way that practically guaranteed approval. *A Japanese Tragedy* (Nihon no Higeki, 1953), though it blamed traditional Japanese values for the fate of the poor mother—after having given up everything for her children, they leave her and she commits suicide—did not attempt to disguise the fact that a motivation of equal power was the vicious new ways which had infected the youngsters.

In *Times of Joy and Sorrow* (Yorokobi mo Kanashimi mo Ikutoshitsuki, 1957) Kinoshita openly supported, and glamorized, the family system. It is the story of a couple who run lighthouses (hence the foreign title, *The Lighthouse*) in various parts of Japan. The end assumption is that staying in relatively uncomfortable living quarters and doing their duty has paid off in all the joys and sorrows that they are, at the end of the film, able to remember. In a picture as late as *The Scent of Incense* (Koge, 1964), a three-hour chronicle film, we see that traditional Japan—reactionary and insular—has a way of warping lives, but that this is somehow beautiful because it enables people to live nobly if (or because) unhappily.

Even more explicit was *The Ballad of Narayama* (Narayamabushi-ko, 1958), about a small community in the northern mountains whose custom it was to expose the aged to the elements so that there would be more food for the young. The barbarity of the custom, one absolutely unauthenticated it should be added, did not move Kinoshita (indeed, he made very decorative use of it) nearly so much as did the spectacle of the son who, the perfect Japanese *chonan*, weeping and struggling, was forced to deposit his mother on top of Narayama. Tradition, in this case, naturally, did not consist of the fictitious abandoning of the aged, but rather the traditional respect with which youngsters regard their elders in Japan, a tradition all the more conspicuous because of its ostensible absence from this film.

Technically *The Ballad of Narayama* reflected Kinoshita's later preoccupation with the traditional. Though using both color and widescreen, the director relied heavily on stage effects—even choosing to frame the story in devices taken from the Kabuki, that most traditional of Japanese theatrical forms. At times this thoroughly conservative motion picture even appeared to be filmed theater.

The same was somewhat true of *The River Fuefuki*

(Fuefukigawa, 1960)—Kinoshita's last important picture before his retiring into television—a chronicle film about five generations in the lives of a poor farming family during the sixteenth century. Again, the film had a rich theatricality about it, emphasized by a use of color which purposely imitated the very early forms of Japanese woodblock prints. In addition Kinoshita, particularly in the battle scenes, used still photographs which both halted and held the action. Though this technique might be described as an innovation, one should also notice its extreme similarity to the *kami-shibai,* the old paper-slide theater which the boys and girls of Japan still love.

The theme of the film would appear antitraditional. The final scene, the true climax of this beautifully made and often compelling film, shows the last remaining member of the family picking up the banner of the ruling family, for which he and his ancestors have traditionally fought, as it floats by on the river, then, with a superb gesture of rejection, throwing it back into the river. What has also become apparent, however, is that Kinoshita is only rejecting the worst. The rest of traditional life he keeps and approves. Perhaps no more war for tyrannical ruling families but, at the same time, when every new son rides off into the world we are made to feel that mother and father are somehow slighted and that, after all, the family is the most important thing. The attitude of a director such as Imai would be, perhaps, that mother is wrong, that it is more important for a young son to realize himself. With this interpretation one feels that Kinoshita would disagree and it is this fact which puts him on the side of the traditionalists.

Not that both views are not equally valid—and Japan is a living proof that they are. It is simply that they are different, but by no means mutually contradictory ways of regarding life. Every person who has ever lived has experienced the problem. At the same time, however, the Japanese finds that, due to the accidents of his history and his temperament, it is dramatized in almost every aspect of his daily life. And in daily life it is perfectly possible for a person to balance within himself the traditionalism of an Ozu and the adventuresomeness of a Kurosawa. The worth of these directors, however—though their true worth is that they both make masterpieces—lies partially in their cogent statements of these apparently opposite points of view.

Japan, as even the most cursory glance will ascertain, is a land of extremes. Perhaps it is for that reason that Japan so dramatizes the search for the compromise which is typical of this century. Since most Japanese live, more or less, by a double standard—that of traditional Japan and that of the West—a compromise becomes not only attractive but even necessary. This search is continually reflected in Japanese films, not only those of Ozu, Naruse, Toyoda, Mizoguchi, Kurosawa, Imai, Yoshimura, Kinoshita, and many others whose predominant concern is to make an honest personal statement which has the widest possible relevance, but also in those films which come and go and in which the director is only concerned in entertaining his audience.

Moreover, such films, simply because their aim is to please, often tell more about a country than its more lasting cinema does. Ozu's films tell a lot about Japanese life in particular but they tell just as much about life in general. The ordinary Japanese film, in that it includes not only Japan as it is but also Japan as the audience would like it to be, gives us an indication of the aspirations of the Japanese audience.

For example, the role of the father in these entertainment films is much less important than one would think, given that the country is officially a patriarchy. Perhaps this is the very reason that popular films cast him in so relatively unimportant a role. All such pictures, while apparently supporting things as they are, at the same time attempt to show us what we want to see and, consequently, cannot but completely if inadvertently criticize an existing order. In Japan the father is important. In principle he is a figure with both stature and dignity. Yet in most Japanese films he is either a figure of tragedy or a figure of fun.

The funny father is seen mostly, as would be expected, in films intended for the young. He, played by such actors as Shuji Sano and Ken Uehara, or by comics like Hisaya Morishige and Frankie Sakai, is often made ridiculous by indulging himself in activities he forbids his own children. He may, for example, keep a mistress while disapproving his daughter's having a boy friend. Quite often one of his most ridiculous qualities is that he is on the children's side—often against mother—and the humor lies in the fall of the main pillar in the family structure. Another favorite complication is that father is more childish than any of the children. The tragic father is always tragic because he is no longer a father and the films of Ozu are, even on this popular level, the perfect example.

Mother, on the other hand, is almost always sympathetic. She is also so prevalent that an entire genre, the *haha-mono,* or mother film, has been created just for her.

In the usual *haha-mono* there is no escape for mother. She must sacrifice and suffer. It is all a part of her life. If she has any happiness, it is only in the hope that her husband may reform. There is very slight chance of this, however; it is not even socially desirable in a totally male-oriented society.

Then there are also problems with the children, who often turn out ungrateful for mother's loving care. In a foreign film, when a child runs away, the mother often feels that she has some connection with her child's departure and that perhaps he will be happier away from home. It seldom occurs to the Japanese mother in the ordinary *haha-mono,* however, that her child's happiness is at stake. She feels totally betrayed and the only remedy is a complete reconciliation in which all the old relationships are restored.

Thus, the foreign film mother finds happiness through adjustment; the Japanese entertainment film mother almost never realizes that any adjustment, other than her child's, is required. Mother's attitude may be unreasonable but, as has been pointed out many times before, she has a vested interest to protect. In Japanese films the highest attainment a woman can reach is not in becoming a wife, as in, say, an American film, but in becoming a mother.

That this rather monstrous mother as seen in Japanese films does not often exist in real life means little. She exists on film and is there because audiences have willed her there. The most notable *haha* is Yuko Mochizuki, a fine actress who now finds herself mother most of the time. She—and this particular type of mother role—is seen at her best in such atypical films as Kinoshita's *A Japanese Tragedy* and Imai's *Rice* (Kome, 1957). In both films she commits suicide, the common lot of Japanese film mothers.

Though mother still reigns, a contender has appeared in the *tsuma-mono,* or wife picture. This is a postwar development and reflects a very real change of Japanese attitude. Of course wives were featured in prewar films but seldom did these pictures focus on them as individuals unless they also happened to be mothers. In such cases the fact that mother is also a wife was irrelevant. To speak of a mother in a *haha-mono* is to speak of a person who occupies a definite place in the family. In the *tsuma-mono,* on the other hand, it is a concern for the wife as an individual which animates the film. Her problems are personally hers and though she may represent young or old wives everywhere, the emphasis is upon her as an individual.

Not that her problems in Japanese films are too varied. Usually this motion-picture wife is concerned with her attempt to defend or discover her own individuality. Very often her problems arise from an empty married life. She thus seeks other ways in which to expand her personality. To do so she must usually fight the old people —traditionally incapable of understanding. Sometimes the plot hinges on the wife's or the husband's inconsequential affair with another person and comes to a climax when both discover their old love for each other.

In Japanese films the most typical wife was the now-retired Setsuko Hara. In fact, if the industry had anything approaching a woman's woman, it would be she. Her approach was almost consistently feminine and her presumably best-loved roles illustrated the idea that occasionally mother, but more often wife, knows best.

The decline of the *haha* and the ascent of the *tsuma* prepares us, to some extent, for what has happened to the daughters in the ordinary Japanese film. Traditionally daughters are unmarried wives, that is, they know their place and they stay there. The majority of Japanese daughters, however, as seen in the Japanese entertainment film, are in revolt. Very often the modernity of the daughter is measured by her outspoken disobedience. There are, to be sure, still "nice" daughters—Kyoko Kagawa, a most talented actress, continued to specialize in these roles until her marriage and consequent retirement —but they are usually pushed into the background or used merely as contrast to those of her more progressive sisters. She, one may be certain, will be at least partially emancipated, she will talk back to mother and father, she will strike out on her own. Sometimes she must pay for her disobedience but, although daughters still return to a forgiving mother and an eventually benevolent father, or still go walking off high buildings or under locomotives, the much more usual pattern involves her being a brilliant success on her own. Since nothing succeeds like success, the spectacle of daughter triumphant on the stage, daughter as head of the women's wear department, daughter in the arms of the company president, always wins over the old folks at home and the films end happily.

This kind of compromise, tradition appeased and individuality attained, is common but at the same time a number of precautions must be taken. Daughter films must appeal to the unformed young, so revolt must be approved. Yet at the same time adults, probably parents themselves, must not be offended. In addition, the Japanese young tend to be a bit more prudish than those in other countries and so the revolt had, until recently, to be made somehow respectable.

One of the solutions to this problem was typically Japanese and very indicative of the audience to which these films are aimed. There was not one heroine but three. Each represented an attitude toward life, and each personified a kind of solution to the problem which plagues the Japanese adolescent. Originally the three were portrayed by Hibari Misora, Chiemi Eri, and Izumi Yukimura.

The last was, culturalogically speaking, to the extreme left. She was by far the most sophisticated, sprinkling her lines liberally with such evidences of foreign culture as English words and passing references to James Dean and Elvis Presley. In the first of these films—for their popularity was such that the idea soon became a series —she had the well-remembered line: "Me in a kimono? I have never worn a kimono in my life."

Chiemi Eri was the slightly comic country type, stocky and well intentioned. She was obviously a pivot between her girl friends. Hibari Misora, representing the extreme right, was always the traditional one. She used not one word of English and her songs and dance numbers were all traditional. No matter how frivolous the others, she stood for reason, duty, obligation, and the most complete respectability. And, in these films, it was she who was promptly rewarded by getting the boy whom they had been squabbling about and having their dream sequences over.

Somewhat later another series of "three-girl" pictures was launched, one built along the same lines but containing many subtle differences. The three girls became Noriko Shigeyama, Sonomi Nakajima, and Reiko Dan. They were no longer called *musume-tachi* as in the other films, but *o-nei-chan-tachi.* These girls were no innocents. The familiar *nei-chan* suggests bars and hotel rooms rather than the ice-cream parlor and school rooms brought to mind by *musume.*

The three resembled, though somewhat superficially, their predecessors. Noriko Shigeyama was further out; she usually had a part-time job dancing in a nightclub. Sonomi Nakajima was, again, the pivot, but was this time much more masculine, her comedy consisting in the main of her using male language and engaging in rough and dangerous sports. She travestied men, something that

Chiemi Eri never did. Reiko Dan had the Misora role but almost everything traditionally Japanese had vanished except that she had the best business head of the three, a talent which she devoted exclusively to thinking up money-making schemes.

Yet social irresponsibility, though shown as a virtue throughout most of these films, is not allowed to triumph. The three girls are brought up to date but, at the very end of each film, we are given indications not that they have realized the error of their ways but that they have found a way to combine the traditional with the individual.

Sonomi Nakajima is shown in kimono, meeting her husband-to-be. It is the traditional arranged marriage. She, to be sure, makes some dreadful error in etiquette or speaks out just when she should be most demure but the point is that she is observing the traditional forms and this quite satisfies any dissenters in the audience. Reiko Dan finds some young man who can make money even better than she can and this leads, naturally enough, to love and marriage. Noriko Shigeyama, about whom the other two have been worrying, turns out to be virtuous after all. She was merely acting loose in order to attract the man with whom she is on the road to matrimony at the final fadeout.

Later, the still-popular three-girl formula was discarded to the extent that the modern young girl (Shima Iwashita, Mariko Okada, etc.) was revealed to be so capricious and eccentric as to include all the facets of the original trio. Consequently, there was, in such young girls, something for everybody (which in terms of Japanese box office more and more came to mean nothing for anyone).

The position of the son in Japanese films is, naturally, just as unlifelike as is that of the Japanese film daughter. If the father is the shivered pillar of the Japanese family, then the son is the slender sapling upon which the entire edifice will eventually lean. He is responsible and is made to feel his responsibility. When the given duty conflicts with personal inclination we then have a collision which has enlivened Japanese literature from the earliest times and which still continues to have the widest application to literature, to films, and to life.

A son or daughter giving up all for the sake of duty is relatively rare in the films, though it occurs often enough in real life. Obviously audiences want to see what they want, and what they want is just as obviously personal gratification. Yet, the Japanese audience is considerably less self-indulgent than some. What it wants, judging from what it likes, is the kind of compromise where gratification may also be approved. The ideal was reached in the films of Yujiro Ishihara—once one of the most popular stars in postwar Japan.

His public was not that of say, the almost equally popular Kinnosuke Nakamura, who appeared only in period films and whose fans were just postadolescent. Nor was it that of the somewhat later Yuzo Kaiyama, son of the matinee idol Ken Uehara, and—as seen in such films as those in the popular *waka-daisho* (young leader) series—given to foreign travel, winning the soccer game for alma mater, and Coca-Cola, all indications of a somewhat affluent, somewhat sophisticated younger audience. Rather, he appealed to those who are slightly older, not yet adult, and just becoming aware of life's little problems.

Superficially there is nothing very distinctive about Yujiro Ishihara. He acts and looks just like his fans, though perhaps unlike them he always seems to have unlimited free time, usually sufficient cash, and he knows some English. Also, he has, for a Japanese, unusually long legs. Equally superficially, he shares with his fans a rebellion against authority, against parents, against the prevailing morality, the Japanese tradition. Yet, unlike them, he also seems to have reached a welcome compromise. One rarely sees him going the whole way. He may dabble in crime—in the early part of his film career—but he never becomes a criminal; he may make uninhibited love yet he rarely gets married; he fights with his parents but never leaves home.

In a typical film one finds that he has disagreed with his parents but rather than leave the house entirely is living in the garage, remaining on terms much less strained than one would think between a father and a son who insists on living in the garage. When his younger brother shows an inclination for the girl he himself wants, he resigns himself to it and the sight of this great traditional virtue in action so impresses the girl that she jilts the brother. He is ultimately successful in everything he does, and his triumph is almost always a moral one: he points to the middle of the road, that position so traditionally happy in Japan. He has found a solution to the problem which plagues his audience, the problem of choice. He chooses both. He has long legs and traditional virtues.

These entertainment films had small connection with Japan as it is and over the years have come to have even less. One may continue to speak with assurance of their patterns because one of the tragedies of the Japanese film industry is that while its audience has changed, the icons and archetypes which it presents have not. The triple-faceted daughter and the traditional long-legged son have now almost no meaning for young Japanese, with the result that films made for this audience no longer reach it. Yet the failing industry is so fearful that it still trots out the aging Ishihara or, better, puts Ishihara and Nakamura in the same film (sometimes adding Toshiro Mifune and another still-popular actor, Shintaro Katsu, as well), vainly hoping that the resulting bargain will lure the largely vanished audience back into the theaters.

If such films are no longer viable indications of contemporary Japanese attitudes, however, they do dramatize the conflicts which are shown in the most mature Japanese cinema. Those films, with a scrupulous regard for accuracy, present Japan as it is, particularly those which are concerned with the traditional.

This quality of the traditional, palpable in the films of Ozu and Naruse, noticeable even in the ordinary *haha-mono*, is, eventually, the creation of that faintly elegiac serenity which the Japanese himself creates with but a hanging scroll and a few flowers, and which the Japanese motion picture likewise creates, using only the simplest of means. Though Japanese films can be crude, violent, and stagy, it is never the majority nor even, perhaps, the larger body of a nation's pictures which contribute toward its cinematic style. Movies belong to the movies and the influence of films on films is international. At the same time, however, different ways of thinking and feeling among peoples accounts for the profile of a national style. We have seen some of these attributes which have resulted in that of the Japanese.

It is possible for the Japanese film to appear long-winded, tedious, clichéd because just as the reading rate and the thinking gait of the country are both slow and safe, the viewing pace is slow. At the same time there is the possibility and often the necessity of a consequent emotional and intellectual understanding which is not invariably present in the hurried West. And here one begins to understand something about the apprehension of mood: one must understand mood in order to feel it; mood, properly, is a product of contemplation.

Just as the Japanese lyric poem is made of a single emotion set to paper, or—as in the *haiku*—a single instance, a solitary happening caused by the collision of two ideas; so, a painting is often that of a single object—bird, branch, mountain. The picture, like the poem, can be and often demands to be an object of contemplation.

So it was once in the West. The picture was conceived precisely as an object to contemplate. One stood and gazed at the still life. The effect was presumed to be much deeper, much more meaningful, than the glimpse of an actual bowl of fruit, an actual bouquet of flowers. Western painting itself began by demanding not only contemplation but—Virgin Mary, Infant Christ—devotion. Now, of course, Western painting has become an act of criticism, but in the East painting retains its traditional role.

One looks long at the mountain or the flower, and what it is—its mood of existence, as it were—is slowly apprehended. *It* is apprehended because contemplation ensures that nothing else is. One either looks at Ozu's single, motionless figure, or is bored. It is presumed (and this is a presumption that Western art, to its loss, no longer makes) that there is something within you, the viewer, which can respond and comprehend. The length of some Japanese films, their lack of movement, their innocence of plot, their richness of atmosphere—these are definite presumptions. The audience, it is presumed, will take advantage of these qualities to create, for itself, a meaningful, emotionally rich experience. Japanese films are sometimes called poetic, and so they are, in the deepest sense. Just as in poetry you pause, seeing the words as though for the first time, set off as each is in its own context, so, in the traditional Japanese film, each scene is meant to be looked at for its own sake. It is meant to be contemplated. It is not a vehicle (not merely a vehicle, at any rate) to carry you from one section of the story to the next. It is to be appreciated for itself.

This is the theme of Asian art. The way in which

context comments on character, in which nature speaks for emotions, a view which both isolates and consolidates —this is the contribution of Asia; in films, the gift of the Japanese.

The traditional view is not the only view of the Japanese director and a concern with traditional problems is not his only concern. Japan is as contemporary as it is traditional, as forward as it is backward looking, as radical as it is conservative. If a concern for the traditional might suggest a similarity among those directors who interest themselves in it, there is, at the same time, the greatest divergence and dissimilarity among those directors who interest themselves in the less traditional aspects of the land and its people.

Naturally, all good directors, traditional or otherwise, are individualists; this is just as true for Ozu, or Naruse, as it is for Kurosawa, Ichikawa, or Shohei Imamura. The only directors who are not individualists are those not seriously interested in making good films. It is quite possible to see Ozu as an individualist; indeed, from one point of view he is a great one. On the other hand, he is committed to a subject matter, to an attitude which, in turn, creates his style. He is certainly just as consistent a stylist as Kurosawa, perhaps even more so since Ozu's pictures are so profoundly similar to each other, and those of Kurosawa are, at least superficially, so different from each other. Yet this style is, in at least part, created by a devotion to a single view; Ozu's perspective is narrow though his penetration is profound. A director like Imai or Shinoda has all the advantages of multiple perspective—each film is different—but, perhaps because of this, each has yet to make a truly personal film. Kurosawa, the complete individualist, is committed to no world view. He is continually experimenting, yet his statement is uniquely his and, while over and over again emphasizing the same ideas, he is, at the same time, interested in the new, the radical, the untried. Ozu cherishes his self-imposed limitations, but Kurosawa will not tolerate limitations. Each has made his quality a strength. One may then arrange Japanese directors on a kind of scale in which Ozu would represent the extreme right, and Kurosawa the extreme left.

If one did so, Mizoguchi would probably fall directly in the middle, since his films partake of both qualities. In a picture such as *Sisters of the Gion* both extremes are present: the elder sister is from a world which Ozu knows well; the younger fits into the world of Kurosawa. In Mizoguchi, particularly in the postwar films, we find a balance, rare in Japanese cinema, between the classic poles of the traditional—the acceptance of feudal values, the affirmation of the home, the joy of submitting to restraint; and the individual—the impatience with restraint, the criticism of all traditional values, the joy of overcoming obstacles, of enlarging horizons.

This becomes apparent if we examine a single, though important, aspect of Mizoguchi's later films: his treatment of women. The director's major theme—and no matter what his Japanese reputation for extreme eclecticism, Mizoguchi's pictures are built, or can be arranged, around a theme—is women, their position or lack of it, their difference from men, their relations with men, the profoundly intricate relations between women and love: this theme is just as much Mizoguchi's as it is Marcel Carné's or George Cukor's.

That most perfect of all his films, *Ugetsu* (Ugetsu Monogatari, 1953), presents the theme in its most perfect form. A potter, caught in the period of civil wars, leaves his wife and small son behind, and goes to sell his wares. There a beautiful lady buys his stock, takes him home, and eventually seduces him. He stays on only to awaken one morning to find both mansion and lady gone. He had been enchanted. Rushing home he finds his wife waiting for him. But the next morning he awakes and discovers that she too was a spirit, and has been dead for some time.

These two women represent the extremes of Mizoguchi's theme: it is much more than simply profane vs. sacred love. Rather, it displays a subtle irony: in the end both women died needing love, the spirit in the haunted mansion is to be equated with the loyal and loving wife. They are equal and it is this parallel that interests Mizoguchi, just as much as did the similar parallel of *Sisters of the Gion* or the parallel conflicts which decide the fate of the heroine in *Osaka Elegy* (Naniwa Hika, 1936).

The point of *Utamaro and His Five Women* (Utamaro o Meguru Gonin no Onna, 1946) is that all, no matter what their superficial differences, are to be equated by their love for the artist. In *Women of the Night* (Yoru no Onnatachi, 1948) and his last completed film *Red-Light District* (Akasen Chitai, 1956—shown abroad as *Street of Shame*) the women, dissimilar in all else, are the same in hunger for love.

Such films contain the extremes of Mizoguchi's attitude; at the same time single movies insist upon one extreme or the other. *The Life of a Woman by Saikaku* (Saikaku Ichidai Onna, 1952—known abroad as *The Life of Oharu*) shows the heroine, Kinuyo Tanaka, falling from court lady to common prostitute and does so with such warmth and delicacy that by implication every one of the feudal institutes responsible for the fall is indicted. In *A Story from Chikamatsu* (Chikamatsu Monogatari, 1954) the woman, played by Kyoko Kagawa, is forced into adultery by the suspicion of it: her jealous husband drives her, innocent, from the house. It is only after this that she becomes guilty. In *Sansho the Bailiff* (Sansho Dayu, 1954), mother and daughter—Kinuyo Tanaka and Kyoko Kagawa—are the true focus of the film. Separated by feudal practice at its most brutal, they are never reunited, and when the son finally discovers his aged, blind mother it is, tellingly, first of her daughter that she asks. In *A Picture of Madame Yuki* (Yuki-Fujin Ezu, 1950), the heroine—played by Michiyo Kogure—commits suicide (that is, is punished) because she cannot accept the new postwar world. Love, for her, is the tact of old-fashioned adultery and not the direct rape of new-fangled marriage. In *The Princess Yang Kwei Fei*

(Yokihi, 1955), the Chinese concubine Machiko Kyo loves her emperor so much that she lives on after death and the final scene shows the aged ruler listening to the sound of her voice.

In all of his films Mizoguchi presented and often reconciled the extremes of attitude we find in Japan. Ordinarily, perhaps, it would be unfair to categorize a director judging merely by the content of his film, content over which most directors have no control. In the case of Mizoguchi, however, as is the rule with most of the best Japanese directors, film content goes far toward describing the personality. Mizoguchi was so eminent that he could choose his own material, and also he usually worked with the same writer, Yoshikata Yoda: the two were just as much a part of each other as were Dudley Nichols and John Ford, as were Noda and Ozu. Too, these extremes are equally well reflected in the technical means through which Mizoguchi achieved his effects.

Basically, Mizoguchi was "old-fashioned" in that he was both literary and painterly. He thought in terms of character rather than camera, and he composed his scenes in a pictorially pleasing manner. To remember a Mizoguchi film is often to remember a series of startlingly beautiful stills: the picnic on the lawn in *Ugetsu;* the boat scene in *A Story from Chikamatsu;* Kinuyo Tanaka calling for her children on the windy promontory in *Sansho the Bailiff;* again, as the aged prostitute sitting in the sun in *The Life of Oharu.* He himself thought of films in the "old-fashioned" manner. He did not like widescreen, much preferring the painting-like ratio. He always referred to movies as *shashin,* a shortened form of *katsudo shashin,* which is a bit like a director referring to the "flickers."

On the other hand he would seek the most experimental means in order to achieve the atmosphere which was for him the essence of the film. Throughout his career he was, for example, interested in the one-scene, one-shot method, one so thoroughly old-fashioned—Griffith dropped it very early in his career—that in the hands of both Mizoguchi and Ozu it appears almost experimental. The climactic scene from *Women of the Night,* for example, is a single shot, one filled with action (a fight among the prostitutes) but all filmed stage-front, as it were. The boat scene in *A Story from Chikamatsu* lasts for several minutes, the camera never moving, never stopping, and the director not once cutting.

This did much to create the atmosphere of the Mizoguchi film, the feeling that this was a real world. Another method was the long shot, in which all action is far from the camera. One remembers, again, the scene on the lawn in *Ugetsu* in which the potter and the lady are almost lost in a field of superlative beauty; the street scenes in *Utamaro* in which the characters are visually joined to their environment; the flight sequence from *Chikamatsu,* the fleeing lovers almost invisible at the bottom of deep ravines, obscured in plains of reeds; the truly lovely scene of the mother, nurse, and children wandering in the marsh of flowering grasses toward the beginning of *Sansho the Bailiff.*

Neither of these methods was, of course, new to the screen, but Mizoguchi pushed them to their extreme limits. Likewise, his consummate use of camera movement became an innovation (never once for its own sake: Mizoguchi was only concerned with the re-creation of a complete atmosphere) simply because of the extremely adventuresome way in which he used it.

In the 1933 *Taki no Shiraito* there is a superb example of controlled camera movement. The scene opens with the autumn sky, the camera moving to a tree and panning down with the leaves as they fall. It watches them gather and then moves smoothly to catch the circus posters being taken down, then moves on, inside the theater, watches the packing, stops to hear one of the characters saying that it is the end, that the season is over. Again, in *Sisters of the Gion*, the opening scene—one long dolly shot—begins the story, illustrates the theme, and introduces the characters. We glide from the street (the milieu) into the shop (the theme: changing ways in 1936 Japan), continue to the rooms at the rear where we find the story already begun and the characters already there.

Perhaps the finest single example is the final scene of *Ugetsu*. The little boy places the offering on his mother's grave and then the camera, with the gentlest, the most reverent of movements, begins to climb, until finally the entire little settlement on the side of the lake is seen in a shot which matches the slow pan from lake to houses of the opening of the film.

It is perhaps typical of the Japanese—it is certainly typical of Mizoguchi—that a known technique, the ability of the moving camera to create atmosphere, should be used with a freedom and a daring rare in the cinema: in film, as in much else, Japan did not invent techniques or even styles; rather, it brought those existing to a point of perfection.

Mizoguchi's individuality, one tempered by his concern for tradition, is matched by that of Heinosuke Gosho. Both insist upon atmosphere but the results are different. The former created atmosphere through his craft, the graphic elements of photography, by camera viewpoint, camera movement. If Mizoguchi had the eye of a painter, Gosho has the eye of a dramatist. The raw material of his pictures, people, what they are and what they do, creates the atmosphere of a Gosho film. While Mizoguchi was interested in the pictorial elements of each photographed scene, Gosho, using editing as a base, is much more interested in the photographed material itself.

Much of the power of Gosho's best films derive from what is shown. A simple example is found in *Growing Up* (Takekurabe, 1955), in the scene where the young heroine, designed from birth for a life of prostitution but never fully aware of it, innocently enters into a conversation with the adults who are deciding her precise fate. A ray of sunlight is illuminating the *shoji* and the shadow of a bird cage is seen against it. But it is not only a symbolic cage, it is also a very real one, our attention having been called to it twice before. We believe in it both as a real object and as a symbol. The scene ends with a closeup of the shadow, the director choosing to make a passing reference to the real meaning of the scene, conveyed in the only possible way through which the idea remains unsentimental.

The danger of sentimentality is ever present in Japanese cinema, and particularly so in Gosho's films: there is always the risk that emotion will be lavished on unworthy objects. But, though he skirts the edge, just before the final plunge something always pulls him up short. In *An Inn at Osaka* (Osaka no Yado, 1954) there is a famous scene in which the inn servant, desperately poor, looks at the crayon drawing of a cow sent her by her son, whom she very much wants to visit. After this very affecting episode comes a scene of ferocious cruelty, involving the callous landlady and the cow drawing, which is followed by a very funny scene showing the landlady's remorse. Then Gosho includes the real heartbreaker when the mother is forced to display her few belongings in the search for a missing thousand-yen note. Their shabbiness is revealed along with the few small toys she has managed to buy for her child, to take to him on a trip which in all probability she will never make. In the resulting conflict of emotion all idea of sentimentality is lost, and Gosho has shown carefully and plainly all of these objects which speak to us so simply and profoundly: the cow, the mother's face, the toys, her hands.

Objects take on life, or at least reflect it. At the end of *Where Chimneys Are Seen*, the husband looks once more at the four factory chimneys, so placed that all four are never visible at once, so that they never appear the same to any two people, and says: "Life is whatever you think it is. It can be sweet or it can be bitter . . . whichever you are." Gosho can use even the most trite symbol, and use it successfully. At the end of *Growing Up* the boy gives the girl an iris blossom—at the beginning he had given her a branch of crepe myrtle—and as she crosses the drawbridge into the house of prostitution, she unthinkingly throws it away, where it lands in a dirty canal. This is a hackneyed symbol which through careful usage manages to regain most of its original urgency.

Another way in which Gosho creates his atmosphere is in his use of numerous closeups and the number and rapidity of his separate shots. As early as 1925 he began using a great number of shots, saying that he was impressed with their importance in Lubitsch's *The Marriage Circle,* a film he saw twenty times and which, along with Chaplin's *A Woman of Paris,* he regards as the greatest foreign influence on his work. *An Inn at Osaka* is composed of over a thousand separate shots, and *Growing Up* has even more. The final reel of Mizoguchi's *Ugetsu,* on the other hand, contains only fourteen. Gosho, indeed, is known as "the director who uses three shots where others use one." There is a beautiful example at the end of *Growing Up* (the original version and not the 1959 reissue which removed over half an hour from the picture). The last ten minutes of the film, the preparation to go into the house of prostitution, are entirely without dialogue. The background score carries a full-scale passacaglia, a continuation of the opening-credit music. To this Gosho freely cuts a number of scenes, all short, all changing, all held together by the music and by a cinematic logic which creates a great final coda, a kind of chaconne on film.

The subject matter of Gosho's films is resolutely anti-traditional. In the early *Dancing Girl from Izu* (Izu no Odoriko, 1935), the two young people must give up each other because society disapproves. The girl in *Growing Up* is forced into the brothel by an unfeeling traditional society. The various tragedies in *An Inn at Osaka* are caused by a traditional greed for money. The heroine of *Elegy* (Banka, 1957) is shown as being normal and healthy in her love for a married man. His reaction, and that of his wife who commits suicide, is traditional and is responsible for the tragedy. The little boy in *Yellow Crow* (Kiiroi Karasu, 1957), also known as *Behold Thy Son,* is shown as perfectly right in rebelling and running away. His parents learn a lesson and at the end of the film are about to reform. In *The Woman from Ozorezan* (Osorezan no Onna, 1965), also known as *The Innocent Witch,* and Gosho's last representative film, a feudal society pushes the girl, played by Jitsuko Yoshimura, into a whorehouse, and a feudal religion kills her when a priest beats her to death trying to exorcise the evil spirits he believes live within her. In *Where Chimneys Are Seen* the husband and wife are prudently waiting until they can afford to have a baby. A series of events convinces them that they must live today for today, and there is neither yesterday nor tomorrow. They will have their baby.

Gosho has said: "The purpose of a film director's life

is to describe the real life around him and create works which express the true feelings of human beings . . . and only if we love our fellow human beings can we create." This generosity of impulse is constantly reflected in his best films. When the hero is finally transferred to Tokyo at the end of *An Inn at Osaka,* he says: "None of us can say he is happy or fortunate, yet things still seem promising . . . we are able to laugh at our own misfortunes, and so long as we can laugh we still have the strength and courage to build a new future." And so it always is in Gosho's films. In contradistinction to those of Ozu and Naruse, even those of Mizoguchi, there is a sense of release. Something has happened: the circumstances remain the same but the outlook has changed and there is room for optimism.

Gosho's generosity of impulse is shared by several other highly individual directors, among them some as otherwise dissimilar as Kurosawa and Imai. It is perhaps the latter which most closely approximates Gosho's position, though Imai goes much further—further than any other major Japanese director—in his complete condemnation of the traditional.

An Enemy of the People (Minshu no Teki, 1946) was about the wartime "oppression of the masses by the capitalists, and labor's heroic opposition to capitalism, militarism, and imperialism." *Blue Mountains* (Aoi Sammyaku, 1949) was about a young love affair condemned by feudalistically minded elders until teachers and fellow students joined the fight on the side of young love. *Until the Day We Meet Again* (Mata Au Hi Made, 1950) showed young lovers destroyed by the war; *And Yet We Live* (Dokkoi Ikiteru, 1951) was again about the exploitation of workers. *Tower of Lilies* (Himeyuri no To, 1953), showing the death of a group of combat nurses during the invasion of Okinawa, put the blame at least partially on "traditional" Japanese "fatalism." *Muddy Waters* (Nigorie, 1953) was about the oppression of women in a modern feudal society; *Here Is a Spring* (Koko ni Izumi Ari, 1955) showed a group of young musicians traveling around the country entertaining farmers, the aged, lepers, all those whom society forgets. The sensational *Darkness at Noon* (Mahiru no Ankoku, 1956) was based upon a real occurrence and assumed the innocence of the hero even before the actual trial; *Rice* (Kome, 1957) again showed the exploitation of the farmers. *The Story of Pure Love* (Junai Monogatari, 1957) was about a young pickpocket, made that way because of society, and his girl friend, slowly dying of radiation disease. *Night Drum* (Yoru no Tsuzumi, 1958), known abroad as *The Adulteress*, was an extremely strong anti-feudal statement. *Kiku and Isamu* (Kiku to Isamu, 1958) was about half-caste children and their plight in an uncomprehending and uninterested society.

A Story from Echigo (Echigo Tsutsuishi Oyashirazu, 1964), like *Night Drum*, was about a man who loses everything by doing what society expects (he kills his wife and murders her seducer). In *When the Cookie Crumbles* (Satogashi ga Kowareru Toki, 1967) Imai took —unlikely choice—the story of the death of Marilyn Monroe, set it in Japan and blamed the traditional materialistic values of his country. In the multipart *River Without a Bridge* (Hashi ga Nai Kawa, 1968–70) he again examined the lives of those whom society attempts to ignore, in this case the still-flourishing outcast class, the *burakunin* or so-called *eta,* and in *A Woman Named En* (En to u Onna, 1971) he again returned to the manifest injustices of the feudal eighteenth century.

Even this partial list leaves no doubt at all as to where Imai's sympathies lie. These are, to be sure, partially conditioned by his political affiliations; on the other hand, however, there can be no doubt of his genuine compassion: though his films also express his political beliefs, Imai is, at the same time, emotionally committed.

Given such antitraditional, even revolutionary content, one might expect a like style: something incisive, brilliant, cold, something like the Russians in the twenties. One would be disappointed: Imai's films are almost without style. His only "style" is found in the content.

He is one of Japan's most eclectic directors—Yoshimura is another—and his individuality lies almost entirely in his protest. What one remembers in an Imai film is never the entirety of the experience—as one remembers the complete emotional impact of *Tokyo Story* or *Ugetsu* or *Rashomon*—but particular scenes which may or may not typify the film as a whole.

It is hard to forget the scene in *Until the Day We Meet Again* (Mata Au Hi Made, 1950) where the young lovers, soon to be destroyed by war—Yoshiko Kuga and Eiji Okada (the actor later to become famous as the young architect in *Hiroshima Mon Amour*)—say good-bye at the station and kiss the window glass which separates them; Chikage Awashima in *Muddy Waters,* smoking a cigarette, looking almost straight into the camera, and remembering what her youth was like; the audience of lepers applauding soundlessly with their stumps after the youth orchestra has performed for them; Yuko Mochizuki as the mother drowning herself in *Rice;* the superb final scene of *Night Drum* where the young husband, beautifully played by Rentaro Mikuni, having satisfied all that a feudal society demands by killing both beloved wife and lover, suddenly realizes that by satisfying society he has destroyed himself.

Unlike other directors of his generation, notably Kinoshita and Kurosawa—who underwent long apprenticeships under directors Yasujiro Shimazu and Kajiro Yamamoto respectively—Imai entered the films completely untrained and even now has no pretension toward more than simple craftsmanship. This does not mean that his films are amateurish or awkward, but it does account for the fact that his best films are those in which he is deeply and personally involved. It also indicates the reasons why Imai's finest films are those with extremely strong scripts: *Until the Day We Meet Again* was based on Romain Rolland's *Pierre et Luce; Muddy Waters,* on the stories of Ichiyo Higuchi; *Night Drum,* on a play of Monzaemon Chikamatsu. Imai himself is of this opinion. Of the first film, he has said: "The scenario was shot sometimes at only one cut a day. I have always made it a point of thinking only about what is important in each scene. The picture owed its success to the solidity of the scenario and the firmness of its framework." When asked why he made so few films, he answered that good scenarios were hard to find; when asked why he did not write them himself, he said that it was as much as he could do to direct them.

Imai's individuality is found in his statement (and it is rare in Japan to find so strong and so personal a statement) and not in the way in which it is phrased. Very early in the director's career he was once shown around the lot by Kimisaburo Yoshimura, then an assistant to Yasujiro Shimazu, who lectured him for half an hour, ending with the opinion that Imai would never make a successful director, adding that "a person like you would be better suited as a movie critic."

In a way Yoshimura was right, but then much the same could be said of Yoshimura himself. Though by no means so critical of society as is Imai, he is just as eclectic and equally dependent upon script quality. Too, his individuality often consists in what he shows rather than in how he shows it.

"We have a poor tradition for making films," he once said: "Japanese fiction after a thousand years still lacks dramatic contruction. It is all *mono no aware;* this naturally reflects over into films . . . The Japanese novel has simply not developed, and films are related to the construction of the novel . . . Our whole trouble is that, despite surface affection, Japanese just don't like new things."

Yoshimura's films are filled with new interpretations of the old. In this he resembles Mizoguchi, a director whom he much admires. He does not search for new subject matter, as do Gosho and Imai, and he is not at all concerned with social "messages"; rather, he remains purposely unselective, adopting a style to fit the peculiar needs of each film. One of Japan's most versatile directors—some say Japan's only really versatile director—Yoshimura can create almost any kind of film.

His specialty, however, if he can be said to have one, is—like Mizoguchi's—his treatment of women. In *Clothes of Deception* (Itsuwareru Seiso, 1951)—a film very much like *Sisters of the Gion*—Machiko Kyo's modern ideas clashed with traditional behavior and eventually got her into trouble. The excellent *Women of the Ginza* (Ginza no Onna, 1955) was completely antigeisha. *Night River* (Yoru no Kawa, 1956), shown abroad as *Undercurrent*, was about a traditional Kyoto girl, played by Fujiko Yamamoto, with modern ideas. In *Night Butterflies* (Yoru no Cho, 1957), yet another version of *Sisters of the Gion*, Fujiko Yamamoto was the traditional bar mistress from Kyoto, and Machiko Kyo, her Tokyo rival. *The Naked Face of Night* (Yoru no Sugao, 1958) was a complete unmasking of the world of the traditional Japanese dance, in which Ayako Wakao, on her way to the top in a ruthless profession, kicks aside her mentor, Machiko Kyo. In his last representative picture, *The House of the Sleeping Beauties* (Nemureru Bijo, 1968) based on the Kawabata novel, he sought—unsuccessfully it is true—to show a quintessence of femininity in the many drugged beauties with whom the elderly hero intimately if platonically sleeps.

Again, like Mizoguchi—and Kurosawa—Yoshimura specializes in that rare genre, the period film which reflects contemporary life. *Ishimatsu at Mori* (Mori no Ishimatsu, 1949) took the famous period hero and showed him as utterly unheroic, and at the same time it was filled with satirical thrusts at the common *jidai-geki* clichés. *A Tale of Genji* (Genji Monogatari, 1952), though not so successful, did justice to the Lady Murasaki, the first "modern" novelist and one whose observations are as psychologically pertinent now as they were in the Middle Ages. The charming *The Beauty and the Dragon* (Bijo to Kairyu, 1955) was a new interpretation of one of the more famous of the Kabuki plays, in which the princess, beautifully played by Nobuko Otowa, was a thoroughly modern, postwar girl. *An Osaka Story* (Osaka Monogatari, 1957), a production originally planned by Mizoguchi and halted by his death, was realized by Yoshimura with a lightness and a grace which would have delighted the elder director.

Yoshimura's attitude in his pictures—as constructive as it is unusual in the Japanese film world—is in essence completely opposed to that of, say, Ozu, whose virtue as a creator rests precisely on what he does with the materials at hand. Yoshimura, proven foe to the status quo, moves restlessly from theme to theme, from subject to subject. He does not consider himself a specialist in anything and prides himself, rightly, upon his ability to create a style to fit the content of a specific film.

This ability is seen in a film such as *A Woman's Testament* (Jokyo, 1960), a three-part omnibus film, the other two sections of which were directed by Yasuzo Masumura and Kon Ichikawa. Yoshimura's portion is distinguished by a stylistic cohesion missing from the other two. Set in modern Kyoto it shows Machiko Kyo as the cold and wealthy owner of a hotel. Little by little she comes to realize that ambition is not enough and that money is not everything. This very slight story was distinguished by a gradual and graceful revelation of character set in a completely atmospheric rendering of the charm that is peculiarly Kyoto's.

Masumura, a pupil of both Daisuke Ito and Kenji Mizoguchi, also owes much to Yoshimura. It was from the latter that he learned the cutting method which distinguishes his films. There is a tendency in Japanese films to play every scene out even after if has made its necessary points. This arises from a traditional evaluation of naturalism, most directors believing that everything they do should be "just like life." Yoshimura, on the other hand, very frequently makes a direct cut right at the high point of one scene, into another scene which is building up. This telescoping of effect, piling one dramatic point quickly on top of another, is a shorthand method of construction which gives his films their unusual pace. Masumura, using precisely the same methods, creates an even livelier film style.

An example is *Warm Current* (Danryu), a picture which Yoshimura made in 1939 and which Masumura remade in 1957. It was about a young doctor, responsible for a small hospital, who must choose between a dedicated nurse and a spoiled rich girl. The Yoshimura version moved swiftly but was filled with careful revelation of character, sustained by an excellent hospital atmosphere. Masumura's version moved at a breakneck speed completely foreign to most Japanese films. One scene was shoved off by another almost before it was done. It is no wonder that many Japanese critics, long used to the perfectly valid but discursive style of an Ozu or a Mizoguchi, should greet the novelty with praise. One of the results of such a style, however, was that the director had almost no time in which to sketch character, and such fast cutting is certainly not conducive to the creation of atmosphere.

Like Imai, and to some extent, Gosho, Masumura tends to be as good as his scenario. His section of *A Woman's Testament* was about a young working class girl, Ayako Wakao, who uses every one of her charms in an attempt to get ahead. She will do anything—there are some biting and very funny "seduction" scenes—in order to get money to go buy more stocks and bonds. The film was distinguished by a number of quietly lethal interludes in the dance hall, at home, and in the bar, where every one of the more elegant conventions surrounding the Japanese traditional maiden was stripped away.

Just as funny was *The Woman Who Touched Legs* (Ashi ni Sawatta Onna, 1960), a remake of the 1926 Yutaka Abe comedy, which had already been remade in 1953 by Kon Ichikawa. Just as scathing was *Love for an Idiot* (Chijin no Ai, 1967), well known in Europe under the title *La Chatte japonaise,* where a perfectly awful modern girl is again fully delineated. The tender and compassionate ending indicates that a literally sadomasochistic marriage has just as much chance of lasting as most. Perhaps Masumura's best in this genre, however, has been *Giants and Toys* (Kyojin to Gangu, 1958), shown abroad as *The Build-Up*, a very fast moving and at times trenchant attack on the advertising racket in Japan and, by implication, all of the values of a traditionally based society. A very slick advertising director takes an unknown girl from the slums and turns her into a national celebrity. The sudden fame ruins her as a person and, at the end, she walks out on him when he needs her most. At times, however, the director's search for a completely individual style leads him into superficialities. The people in *The Precipice* (Hyoheki, 1958), a mountain-climbing adventure story, never come to cinematic life. *A Man Blown by the Wind* (Karakkaze Yaro, 1960) was a superficial gangster film which marked the acting debut of the late Yukio Mishima. Nor are the two girls in love with each other (Ayako Wakao and Kyoko Kishida) in *Manji* (1964) fully realized characters.

Unlike Yoshimura, whose concern, first, foremost, and always, is for people, Masumura, like some American directors and many Italians (he studied at the Centro Sperimentale in Rome), is often primarily concerned with action. The action in *Nakano Army School* (Rikugun Nakano Gakko, 1966), a beautiful reconstruction of the famous wartime spy school and its fascinating activities, is subdued but powerful, particularly when the hero (the late Raizo Ichikawa) finds that in serving his country he has left himself little to live for. Or the action may be direct, physical, and overpowering—as in Masumura's finest picture, *The Hoodlum Soldier* (Heitai Yakuza, 1965), a film so popular that it later became a series. This story of two soldiers who, for entirely different reasons, hate the army, is filled with blood and laughter, torture and horseplay, and is so cynical about national ideals that for a time there was talk of its not being released abroad. Japanese humor has never been blacker than in this uproarious and disturbing picture, and action—the celebrated fight in the bathhouse scene, for example—has rarely been shown in so powerful a manner.

At the same time, however, one must admit that Masumura is no better than his script and he will, with little discrimination, bring to a picture which neither needs nor wants such bravura precisely those techniques that distinguish a *Hoodlum Soldier* but ruin a lesser vehicle. At the same time, Masumura is among the last first-rate directors to be bound by a company contract which gives him no control over his material. He is continually saddled with the most unprepossessing scripts and is hedged in with conditions from which other good directors have now largely escaped—by forming their own companies or by becoming independent producers.

With Masaki Kobayashi, the concern for action is tempered by a very real concern for social criticism, one which he shares with such directors as Akira Kurosawa and Hiromichi Horikawa. His *Thick-Walled Room* (Kabe Atsuki Heya, 1953), based on published abstracts from the diaries of "war criminals," had as its theme the idea that most of those imprisoned were innocent while the real criminals escaped. Though the theme was perhaps debatable, still, this was one of the few Japanese films to raise the question of responsibility for the war. *I'll Buy You* (Anata Kaimasu, 1956) was another exposé, this time of the commercialization of the Japanese baseball world, with rival teams outbidding each other for the services of a high-school star.

Among the most highly critical of Japanese standards was *Black River* (Kuroi Kawa, 1957), which had as its subject the corruption centering on American bases in Japan. A lively exposition which might easily have been a static indictment, the film was studiously just in its conclusions. The villain was not America for the presence of her camps, but the Japanese social system which permitted lawlessness to go unpunished and even officially unnoticed. Particularly brilliant was the final reel of this film. It is a rainy night and the jerry-built bars and pinball parlors, cheap restaurants and souvenir shops which have grown around the camp entrance look like a deserted amusement park. The young gangster, played by Tatsuya Nakadai, now dead drunk, is being taken home by the girl, Ineko Arima, whom he has seduced and who is now his mistress. There is an argument and he races off down the long, rain-slicked highway. Along the road comes a convoy of American trucks. He slips in front of one of these and is killed. The girl drops her open umbrella and rushes toward him; the final shot shows the umbrella on the highway while she, crying, runs toward the now stationary trucks. The entire sequence, extremely ironic in the film's context, is made up of short shots, gathering momentum to stop abruptly on the long-held final image.

Among the best known of Kôbayashi's films is the massive three-part chronicle of the Second World War, *The Human Condition* (Ningen no Joken, 1958–61), variously known as *No Greater Love, The Road to Eternity, A Soldier's Prayer, Il N'y pas de plus grand amour, Un Destin humaine,* and *Barfuss durch die Hölle.* The picture, scripted by Zenzo Matsuyama, covers Jumpei Gomikawa's best-selling six-volume novel in three-hour parts. It was probably the first postwar war film to show the Japanese army as it actually was. Inevitably, it became one of the most controversial productions ever made in Japan.

Through its criticism of the army, the film—by extension—comments on the entire Japanese system of organization. The young intellectual hero, played by Tatsuya Nakadai, is appalled by the conditions in Manchuria, particularly by the brutal policy of slave labor. He fights against it and is sent into active duty. The remaining two films follow his adventures up to his eventual death. Though impressive in part, the film as a whole is more interested in society than it is in people. Just as Masumura sacrifices character to action, so Kobayashi—a pupil of Kinoshita, and by extension, Shimazu—slights character in favor of social comment.

This is certainly true of films such as *The Inheritance* (Karamiai, 1962), *The Youth of Japan* (Nihon no Seishun, 1968), also known under the title *Ballad of a Tired*

Man, and the overpraised if decorative *Kwaidan* (Kaidan, 1965). But it is not true of *Rebellion* (Joiuchi, 1967), also known as *Samurai Rebellion,* and *Harakiri* (Seppuku, 1962), Kobayashi's single finest film. Here logic is not sacrificed to action nor people to plot, and social comment is relevant to both story and theme. The splendid script is by Shinobu Hashimoto, who also worked on *Rashomon* and directed a single film, the noteworthy *I Want to Be a Shellfish* (Watashi wa Kai ni Naritai, 1959). The story of *Harakiri* concerns a samurai (Tatsuya Nakadai again) who, having seen his son forced to disembowel himself under the cruelest of circumstances, sets out to kill the man he thinks responsible (Rentaro Mikuni). He discovers that it is not the man but the system that is responsible—a system which, then as now, is integral to the traditional Japanese way of life.

Even more critical of Japan is the younger Nagisa Oshima who, in early films such as *A Story of the Cruelty of Youth* (Seishun Zankoku Monogatari, 1960), also known as *Naked Youth,* and *The Tomb of the Sun* (Taiyo no Hakaba, 1960) preferred to dwell upon the more sensational aspects of modern untraditional behavior, to approve the revolt, and to spend more time over a careful delineation of excess than over any treatment of character. Later, his films became political exercises, somewhat in the manner of those of Godard, and it was not until much later that he made a major personal statement with *Death by Hanging* (Koshikei, 1968).

This film, says Oshima, "was suggested by a news story. The real incident took place in 1958 and has been the subject of a lot of works, novels and such. But none of them appeared to go into it deeply enough to reveal the core, the inside of the crime." A young Korean had murdered a young Japanese schoolgirl. Oshima had taken the side of Koreans (against whom the Japanese are almost universally prejudiced) before, and upon the publication of the youth's letters found that "he wasn't guilty of his sin at all." At least, says Oshima, he was not ethically guilty. His point was that law is not possible without crime and that policemen are unimaginable without criminals. There is an unassailable logic in the condemned Korean's observation, upon being warmly assured that it is indeed very bad to kill, that "then it is bad to kill me."

In order to prove his guilt to him in the film, the police set out to re-enact the crime—each one playing a role. This device finds them first imitating the rape and the murder before the uncomprehending eyes of the youth, and then going back to pantomime his earlier life—or, rather, their idea of what his early life was like. Being, first, Japanese, and, second, cops, their idea of childlife in a Korean section is bizarre indeed and Oshima skillfully underlines both the comedy of their lack of imagination and the horror of their lack of comprehension. This inept pantomime alienates to the extent that we understand the irony of this crime within a crime within a crime, the latter being capital punishment itself. The police, says the film, are more obsessed with the idea of crime than any criminal is. Consequently, from a misguided wrongdoer they literally create the role of criminal. This is brilliantly displayed when one of the police, carried away, attempts to kill. He is so intent upon creating a role that he assumes it completely.

A year later (with several films between—Oshima is an extremely prolific filmmaker) he made another major movie, *Boy* (Shonen, 1969). This picture was also based upon something that actually happened: a man and wife had taught their child to run in front of moving automobiles and get hit; they would then rush up and collect damages: in this way they moved all over Japan during 1966, making a fairly good living until finally caught. "It made headlines in magazines and newspapers for one week, and was then completely forgotten," says Oshima. "However, the incident was so shocking that I did not forget it." Later, he said that "though I have taken an objective view, I have also made the film as a prayer, as are the boy's tears in the final scene, for all human beings who find it necessary to live in a like manner." And it is true that, in this sense, the plight of the child is the plight of us all.

That Oshima can make one believe this, particularly given the nature of his material—that much-used fable of the mistreated child—indicates his resources as a director. Rather than following its, and our, inclinations, however, Oshima continually and purposely works against the grain, refusing himself any emotional, let alone sentimental gestures. The little boy is matter-of-fact, the way little boys are. His incredible situation is accepted in the way that children accept enormities. Further, Oshima refuses to avail himself of the symmetry which fables, as such, seem to demand. The form, rather, is organic; it is that demanded by the characters rather than the plot. Open-ended sequences, visual non-sequiturs, and lapses of continuity, all carefully judged, create the air of believability so characteristic of this film. Though far different from such early films about children as those of Ozu and Shimizu, it joins them through its honest realism and its bitter perception.

Equally perceptive were *Ceremony* (Gisaku, 1971), and, in particular, *The Man Who Left His Will on Film* (Tokyo Senso Sengo Hiwa, 1970), an elaborately self-referential film about a student making a movie. He kills himself at the end of the picture, and the film he was making becomes the film we have been seeing. Using a completely amateur cast, Oshima succeeded brilliantly in creating a visual counterpart for the world which an acutely sensitive youth must feel and fear. In these later and mature films the excesses of youth, its revolts, its retreats, are captured with a compassion quite missing from the earlier work.

At the same time, however, one must add that the individuality of Oshima, of Kobayashi, and of Masumura is a bit like that of Imai, and is different from that, say, of Ozu or Kurosawa, in that stylistic unity is imposed not by the director but by the subject matter he chooses.

Another example would be Yasuke Chiba, whose personal style was based entirely in the *shomin-geki* genre seen in the films of Shimazu, of Ozu, or Gosho. *Downtown* (Shitamachi, 1957) was an excellent short film about a poor working woman—beautifully played by Isuzu Yamada—who finds love with a truck driver (Toshiro Mifune) only to lose it when he is accidentally killed. Chiba's finest work was found in the tetralogy *Oban* (1957–58) about a large young man whose ambitions are equally big. (Both of the English titles sometimes used, *Large Size* and *Mr. Fortune Maker,* are not precise: *oban* is an Osaka word, now somewhat quaint, used to designate, not the boss of a company, but the man just under him.) He is a go-getter of the mythological American (or Osakan) variety whose constant energy in life and business is completely foreign to the traditional social ideals of the Japanese. There is no plot as such; the story is a Balzac-like chronicle of the hero's various rises and falls. The richness of character and detail and the many early-1920s touches create throughout all four films an almost palpable atmosphere, one to which Daisuke Kato adds greatly in his perfect interpretation of this César Birotteau transplanted to Tokyo.

Chiba's limitations were the limitations of the genre in which he chose to excel. Now, in this age of affluence, there are no more *shomin* and consequently no more such *geki* and Chiba has long had to resign himself to being merely one of the many house directors of his studio.

Another casualty of his times was Ko Nakahira. He may not have achieved Masumura's brilliance nor Kobayashi's singleness of purpose, nor Oshima's breadth, but he contributed other qualities, such as a lightness one does not often associate with Japanese pictures and a willingness to experiment. His debut film, *Crazed Fruit* (Kurutta Kajitsu, 1956), known abroad as *Juvenile Pas-*

sion), was intended as merely another in the then-current series of juvenile delinquency films, but Nakahira made a picture which sacrificed very little to sensationalism, had an integrity of its own, and was a very moving film experience.

The film concerned two brothers who perhaps simultaneously and certainly repeatedly enjoy the favors of the same girl. Nakahira caught the atmosphere of a second-rate summer resort, the hesitant arrogance of adolescents, the animality of the young, and the setting of the shining sea and sun-drenched beaches. The triangle is completely unconventional: after the girl and the younger brother have met, the elder brother appropriates her, not so much because he wants her as because he does not like to see his younger brother mixed up with her. The ties between the boys are stronger than their ties with the girl, however, and throughout the film there are indications that the younger brother is not so much jealous of his own brother as he is of the girl.

Like the young people in George Stevens' *A Place in the Sun* (a film which much influenced this one—to the extent of having a shot in common: the radio on the pier scene), the youngsters may be cruel and stupid and vicious but it is only because they have neither the energy nor the imagination to be anything else. They are, after all, adolescents, just now awakening into adulthood.

Nakahira's lightness and flair for comedy is seen in *The Four Seasons of Love* (Shiki no Aiyoku, 1958) in which, like Keisuke Kinoshita before him, he showed

Women of the Ginza, 1955. Directed by Kimisaburo Yoshimura. Nobuko Otowa (center).

The Harp of Burma, 1956. Directed by Kon Ichikawa. Shoji Yasui.

Early Spring, 1956. Directed by Yasujiro Ozu. Ryo Ikebe, Chikage Awashima, Chishu Ryu.

Red-Light District, 1956. Directed by Kenji Mizo-guchi. Machiko Kyo, Aiko Mimasu, Ayako Wakao, Kumeko Urabe, Sadako Sawamura, Eitaro Shindo.

A Cat, Shozo, and Two Women, 1956. Directed by Shiro Toyoda. Kyoko Ka-gawa, Chieko Naniwa.

Flowing, 1956. Directed by Mikio Naruse. Seiji Miya-gawa, Sumiko Kurishima, Kinuyo Tanaka.

Black River, 1957. Directed by Masaki Kobayashi. Ineko Arima.

The Throne of Blood, 1957. Directed by Akira Kurosawa. Toshiro Mifune (center).

Snow Country, 1957. Directed by Shiro Toyoda. Ryo Ikebe, Keiko Kishi.

The Lower Depths, 1957. Directed by Akira Kurosawa. Bokuzen Hidari, Akemi Negishi, Kyoko Kagawa, Minoru Chiaki, Eijoro Tono.

Oban, 1957–58. Directed by Yasuke Chiba. Daisuke Kato.

Night Drum, 1958. Directed by Tadashi Imai. Rentaro Mikuni, Ineko Arima.

Enjo, 1958. Directed by Kon Ichikawa. Raizo Ichikawa (left).

The Human Condition, 1958–61. Directed by Masaki Kobayashi. Tatsuya Nakadai.

Floating Weeds, 1959. Directed by Yasujiro Ozu. Hiroshi Kawaguchi, Ganjiro Nakamura.

Fires on the Plain, 1959. Directed by Kon Ichikawa. Eiji Funakoshi, Mickey Curtis.

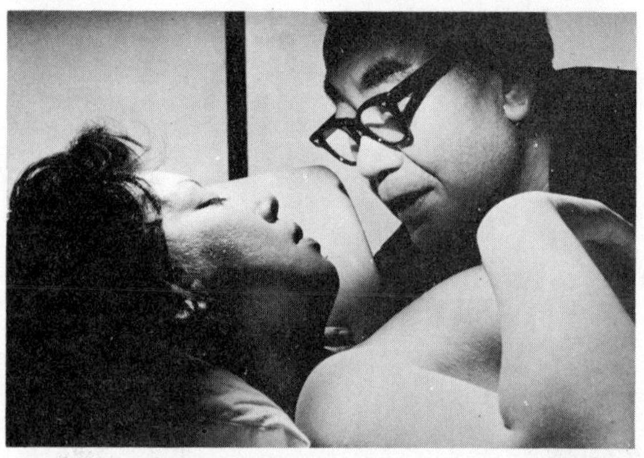

The Key, 1959. Directed by Kon Ichikawa. Machiko Kyo, Ganjiro Nakamura.

Cruel Stories of Youth, 1960. Directed by Nagisa Oshima. Yusuke Kawazu, Miyuki Kuwano.

The Island, 1960. Directed by Kaneto Shindo. Nobuko Otowa.

The Assignation, 1960. Directed by Yasushi Nakahira. Takao Ito, Yoko Katsuragi.

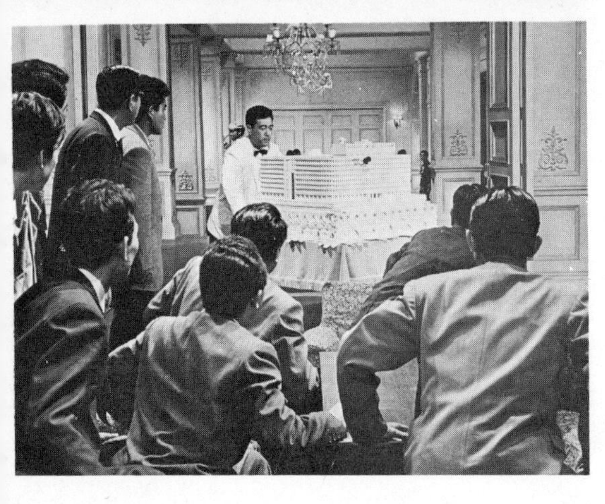

The Bad Sleep Well, 1960. Directed by Akira Kurosawa.

The River Fuefuki, 1960 Directed by Keisuke Kinoshita. Tomohiko Tamura, Hideko Takamine.

Late Autumn, 1960. Directed by Yasujiro Ozu. Setsuko Hara, Yoko Tsukasa, Chishu Ryu.

Bonchi, 1960. Directed by Kon Ichikawa.

Black Book, 1960. Directed by Hiromichi Horikawa. Keiju Kobayashi.

When a Woman Ascends the Stairs, 1960. Directed by Mikio Naruse. Hideko Takamine (center).

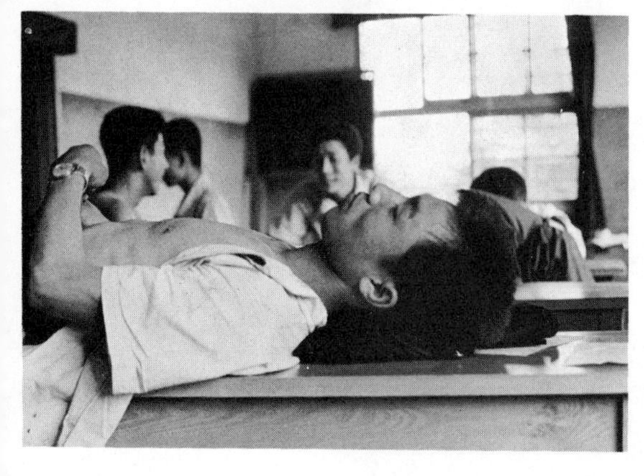

Bad Boys, 1960. Directed by Susumu Hani.

The End of Summer, 1961. Directed by Yasujiro Ozu. Setsuko Hara, Yoko Tsukasa.

Ten Dark Women, 1961. Directed by Kon Ichikawa. Eiji Funakoshi (left), Keiko Kishi and Fujiko Yamamura (right).

Yojimbo, 1961. Directed by Akira Kurosawa. Toshiro Mifune.

Pigs and Battleships, 1961. Directed by Shohei Imamura. Hiroyuki Nagato, Takeshi Kato, Tetsuro Tamba.

Pitfall, 1962. Directed by Hiroshi Teshigahara. Hisashi Igawa.

A Full Life, 1962. Directed by Susumu Hani. Ineko Arima.

Sanjuro, 1962. Directed by Akira Kurosawa. Tatsuya Nakadai, Toshiro Mifune.

Harakiri, 1962. Directed by Masaki Kobayashi. Akira Ishihama.

An Autumn Afternoon, 1962. Directed by Yasujiro Ozu. Kyoko Kishida, Keiji Sada, Chishu Ryu.

that the Japanese family system has almost unlimited comic possibilities. This wryly funny film shows the conservatism of the new generation when compared with their parents.

The children all think that mother—beautifully played by Isuzu Yamada—should stay at home, should give herself up to self-sacrifice, gentleness, and tears. In this they get little cooperation, since their mother is quite determined to lead her own life. The children, puritans all, are aghast. They are not themselves above suspicion, but they keep their little affairs secret and are suitably ashamed. At the end of the film, they are assembled at the railway station; mother, they think, has seen the error of her ways and is returning. They prepare suitable faces, hurt but brave, as the train pulls in. Mother is on it all right, but she is not alone. She is with a gentleman friend on her way to a hot spring resort. The children are horrified. Mother smiles sweetly, the whistle blows and the train moves off. The children are left looking after it, aware for the first time that they are left out, and are missing something.

In *The Assignation* (Mikkai, 1960), a hour-long film, Nakahira shows what he can do with a straight romance. The opening is particularly well done. This is a six-minute sequence without cuts, one long scene, showing a married woman and her lover, a young student, lying on the ground in a deserted park. The scene is so intimate as to be almost embarrassing, yet Nakahira confines himself entirely to the single setup, both actors cut at the waist; the suggestive quality lies entirely in the acting and in the slow, sinuous movement of the camera itself. Later, at the end of the film, the wife, fearful of disclosure, impulsively pushes the student under a train. Here, as in the final motorboat crash in *Crazed Fruit,* Nakahira uses a convincing impressionistic technique, creating his action through a number of extremely short shots: closeups of the two faces, of the wife's hand, the student's foot slipping, his body turning as he falls, the train above them. Finally, we see the train overshooting the station and then the track: a very long-held shot of the student, dead, just head and shoulders at one side of the frame and at the other, at an impossible angle, his foot.

Nakahira, at one time one of the most talented of young directors, was also under contract to one of the most inflexible of the five major film companies (the same company that allowed the brilliant young Kazuo Kawabe to make one film, *Juvenile Delinquents* [Hiko Shonen, 1964], a beautiful near-documentary feature, and then never permitted him to make another). Put to work on one ephemeral entertainment picture after another, and unable or unwilling to escape into an independence where he might be more creative if less secure, he was then sent to Taipei to direct equally undistinguished Chinese entertainment films. Eventually he was able to escape into independent production, with *The Demons of Darkness* (Yami no Naka no Chimimoryo, 1971).

Those directors who left their original companies, or those who were never affiliated with any single company, have done much better. Among them, the one most independent, and the one best known abroad is Susumu Hani.

Son of a very famous liberal, born into a family known for its efforts for progressive education, the young Hani created a fine series of shorts—*Children in the Classroom, Children Who Draw, Horiyuji, Twin Sisters*—before making his first feature, the excellent *Bad Boys* (Furyo Shonen, 1960). In this picture about reform school life he chose his cast from those boys who had already served their time, took them back into the school, and had them reconstruct their life for him. Starting with no story at all, he gradually built up a series of situations —fighting official opposition all the way—and in the end created a film both perceptive and honest about a section of the population about which Japanese society, as do most, finds it expedient to be uninformed.

While the boys were sometimes told what such-and-such a situation was, the dialogue was their own, as was the "acting." Hani discovered that eventually the camera was ignored and that the various scenes naturally disclosed themselves before him. They were "disclosed" and the nonactors were indeed "acting," however, because one of the stipulations of the governmental authorities was that no actual prisoners could be used.

The boys fell back into their old reform school ways at once, Hani has said, but with a difference. This difference was that they were reliving their own lives. This gave the film a deliberate quality. It made the boys thoughtful. While they did not consider their actions, they seemed to be considering the consequences which, naturally, they already knew. This attractive ambivalence led to the final scene of the film—that startling, honest, yet mysterious scene where the leading boy, finally to be released, stands in the hall of the prison and thanks it.

Hani's next feature, *A Full Life* (Mitasareta Seikatsu, 1962), used actors, but he continued to direct them as though they were amateurs, and in this way drew from the popular screen heroine Ineko Arima a performance she has yet to better. She plays a typical, rootless city girl who goes from one man to the other, yet always keeps her self-respect. This is not enough for the full life she imagines for herself, however. Eventually she finds herself through devotion to a man older than herself. She finally allows herself to be completely female, completely herself, and the fine final shot, a very long closeup, finds her happy in behaving the way that all Japanese housewives behave, but with the difference of knowing it and accepting it.

She and He (Kanajo to Kare, 1963) used the same theme, a woman's discovering herself, but now there was no solution. The wife (Sachiko Hidari, whom Hani had married shortly before) is happy with her husband (Eiji Okada) but this is somehow not enough. Again there is a long final closeup at the end as she lies in bed, gazes into the darkness, half-afraid, half-hopeful. This theme again appears in *Bride of the Andes* (Andes no Hanayome, 1966) in which a mail-order bride straight from Japan (Sachiko Hidari again) sees that she must somehow find herself in the wilds of Peru. She succeeds admirably through a combination of toughness, trust, and trying again and again.

Hani's women, perfectly understood and beautifully presented, are seemingly far from those of Mizoguchi or Yoshimura, yet there are similarities of attitude among the directors. All of them would agree that the Japanese woman is the perfect symbol for a problem which is presented to all of us: how to learn to become yourself. Mizoguchi's women largely fail; Hani's women largely triumph, but the problem—one of philosophical dimensions and one peculiarly of our time—is the same.

It is Hani's single theme and a most important one. When he strays from it—*Slave of Love* (Aido, 1969), *Grand Adventure of Love* (Koi no Daiboken, 1970)—he strays completely. When he illustrates it, his films succeed admirably. *Children Hand in Hand* (Te o Tsunagu Kora, 1962), a remake of a 1948 Hiroshi Inagaki film based on an earlier Mansaku Itami script, is about a group of children in a small provincial capital. One of them, a slow and backward child, eventually comes to realize his limitations and, hence, his possibilities. This beautifully detailed picture contains some of Hani's most evocative pictures of childhood. One of them—the children playing some mysterious and almost sinister game of their own devising, in the growing dusk of a house at sunset—particularly illustrates Hani's lifelong love and admiration for the films of Jean Vigo.

The hero of *The Song of Bwana Toshi* (Buana Toshi no Uta, 1965) is a perfectly ordinary Japanese in extraordinary circumstances in the heart of Central Africa.

More even than the German, the Japanese carries his own culture and his own prejudices around with him. A Japanese bereft of both, as Toshi eventually is, is no Japanese at all. He is, as Hani shows, a human being, like all others, and the moral of the film—if it can be said to have one—is that one, after all, learns to be human. That the film is not plotted is one of its strengths. It purposely rambles and among its casual disclosures are some very fine and Hani-like scenes: Toshi and his native friend up a tree baying for hippopotami; the excitement and awe of the natives turning on an electric light for the first time; and the singing and dancing finale with Toshi pleased, embarrassed, sad, happy, and very human.

In some ways Hani's best and in all ways his most typical film is *The Inferno of First Love* (Hatsukoi Jigoku-hen, 1968)—shown in Europe complete and in America much butchered under the title *Nanami.* An adolescent boy and girl meet and agree to sleep together. She has had some experience, he has had none. Before this can occur, however, he is killed. This is the fable which Hani has cast in the form of a contemporary fairy tale, making certain however that the realism of the picture all but hides its mythical overtones. The boy lives in Ueno, that old-fashioned section of modern Tokyo over which still hovers the aura of old Edo. She, on the other hand, lives and works (as a nude model) in glittering, glamorous Shinjuku, one of the great night towns of the world. Hani brings both people and both worlds together in a very skillful reverse reading of one of the oldest of fairy tale patterns (it occurs in the Sleeping

Beauty story, for example) to illuminate a touching and delicate parable of innocence and experience.

This theme is central to all of the best Hani picture because it is this voyage—one we all suffer—from innocence to experience which is traced by almost all of the characters in his films on their way to self-realization. In *The Inferno of First Love,* the theme finds its central statement in the desperate sincerity of the young people (consummately directed nonprofessionals) and the wide range of human experience (for the picture contains everything from masturbation to prostitution, from harmless madness to the most explicit sadism) which threatens to engulf both them and their immature but precious ideas about themselves. At the same time Hani sidesteps an equally threatening sentimentality by the harshness of his photography, by a nervous, prying camera, by refusing any but actual locations, and by the tact and grace with which he directs his young people. As a major statement of a major theme (though a cunningly dissembled one), this film quite deserved the enormous critical and popular acclaim it received in Japan.

It was largely the West that acclaimed *Woman in the Dunes* (Suna no Onna, 1964), the work of Hiroshi Teshigahara, a younger director who had made his feature-film debut shortly before with *Pitfall* (Otoshiana, 1962). *Woman in the Dunes,* scripted as are all of Teshigahara's films by the novelist Kobo Abe, was to prove his most successful. Also a parable—perhaps even an allegory—it is about a school teacher on an outing imprisoned by the local folk in a large sand pit with a recently widowed woman. His attempts to escape are all unsuccessful, and he eventually discovers a way to make potable the water which seeps from the sand. In this way he discovers himself, his purpose, his life, and when the chance finally comes to escape, he refuses it.

This theme of the discovery of identity shares much with the central theme of the films of Hani, but Teshigahara's way of illustrating it is quite different. Early a maker of documentaries—the best example of which is the later motorcar-race film *Bakuso* (1967)—Teshigahara combines great technical skill (extreme depth of focus, immaculate detail, and a somewhat elaborately choreographed camera movement) with a very precise fidelity to his script. This is another way, of saying, of course, that the weaknesses in Teshigahara's later pictures are those of the script itself.

Though Kobo Abe is one of Japan's most able novelists he is not one of its greatest screen writers. Thus, though all of Teshigahara's feature pictures have been based on very successful Abe novels, the author's scripts are, with the exception of that for *Woman in the Dunes,* far less satisfactory. *The Face of Another* (Tanin no Kao, 1966) and *The Burned Map* (Moetsukita Chizu, 1968), also known as *The Man Without a Map*), share with the earlier picture the theme of a search for identity. In the former, a man loses his face in an explosion and has a new one made for him. In the latter, a detective eventually unwillingly assumes the identity of the missing man for whom he is searching. But neither of these approaches the power of *Woman in the Dunes*. The Abe-Teshigahara short multiscreen film *Two Hundred Forty Hours in a Day* (Ichinichi Nihyaku-yonjuji-kan, 1970) is even feebler in conception.

Teshigahara himself has said that he believes his talents are mainly those of a cameraman and while this is overly modest, it is certainly true that the documentary-like realism is the best thing about his feature films. Teshigahara's straight documentaries—such as the multiscreen *Water of Life* (Seimei no Izumi, 1970), completed by Yukio Tomizawa—are excellent indeed.

Another director who has developed his own style of documentary-like realism is Shohei Imamura. Originally he made a number of popular feature films, of which *Pigs and Battleships* (Buta to Gunkan, 1961), a ferocious picturization of life around the U. S. Naval Base at Yokosuka, is probably the most representative. He then went on to create such films as *The Insect Woman* (Nippon Konchuki, 1963) and *Intentions of Murder* (Akai Satsui, 1964).

With *The Pornographer* (Jinrui Gaku Nyumon, 1966), however, his style assumed a new brilliance. Always interested in creating the feeling of realism on the screen he began in this film to capture it through the use of actual locations and completely atypical casting. Imamura had long been fascinated with those whom society officially forgets, such as the pimps and whores around a naval base, or the ignorant and superstitious peasants deep in the country. In this film he denied himself the often easy sentimentality of an Imai and began an earnest investigation of these people. His attitude is shown in an exact translation of the Japanese title of *The Pornographer—An Introduction to Anthropology*. This does not, indicate, however, the smiling irony of the director's investigations nor the extent of his compassion.

The pornographer is an Osaka man who little by little comes to feel that he has a duty in this life. It is to restore to men some of those things that civilization has denied them. First on his list of things to repatriate comes pornography, which he quite plausibly finds hurts no one and pleases many. To this end he sets up an elaborate if homemade studio and begins a thriving business manufacturing blue films. We are treated to scenes of the making of several and these must rank as some of the funniest sequences ever to appear in a Japanese film. Later on he moves to procuring and, toward the end of the film, is much taken with the idea of manufacturing the perfect sexual mate—a life-sized latex doll into which he is busily engaged in imbedding real hair. While working away in his houseboat home, the mooring line slips loose and in a final scene of very mysterious beauty, he sails, all unknowing, through the canals of Osaka and out onto the Pacific Ocean—presumably never to be heard of again.

Immaculately constructed, shot almost entirely on location in Osaka, with a perfect performance by Shoichi Ozawa in the title role, this film indicated the direction that Imamura was to take. It is a deft mixture of logic, compassion, and controlled realism. In *A Man Vanishes* (Ningen Johatsu, 1967) he went even further. Using only a small crew and no "cast," as such, he set out to explore the reality of what happened to a single one of those surprisingly many who (for one reason or another) simply vanish into this small but overcrowded country. Filming as he went, he looked up all of the man's friends, his relatives, his employers, his acquaintances, his girl friend. Inviting her to accompany him, he searched all possible leads, finally picked the one he thought most fruitful, and—in the final reels of the film—practically accuses another woman of the murder (possible only in such a libel-lawless country as Japan). One feels that the man simply disappeared for his own convenience (every year numbers of such vanished folk are discovered living under assumed names and new identities). Thus, one might argue with the director's ultimate intentions. At the same time there is no arguing with the effect of this film. It is more than realistic. It is real. At the same time —and in this Imamura is very Japanese—he is continually touching up this reality. There is one astonishing scene in which he has invited several "suspects" (and us) to a small restaurant. We follow the guests there, through a maze of alleys, sit down with them, and listen to the evidence. Then, with great flair, to make his point about the nature of reality (which is what the restaurant conversation has been partially about), Imamura gives a signal and the roof of the restaurant is slowly raised, the walls slowly come apart. We are in the middle of a vast film studio in which this small restaurant set had been constructed. What the guests (and we ourselves) had taken for reality is pure illusion.

The interchange between reality and illusion—a theme

as central to Imamura as it is to Kurosawa, though in a different manner—is seen again in *A Postwar History of Japan* (Nippon Sengoshi, 1970). Here a woman who lived through these years watches official newsreels covering the same period. Her lively comments and the scenes shown on film widely diverge as Imamura (himself again on screen) prods away to get at a final truth which always eludes, for the simple reason that it does not exist.

In his most interesting film, *Kuragejima: Tales from a Southern Island* (Kamigami ni Fukaki Yokubo, 1968), Imamura shows that it is not only one's own attitude toward reality which changes, but that reality itself can change. It is nearly three hours in its original version, and was filmed entirely on location at Ishigakishima, one of the southern Ryukyus. This picture is an at times uneasy but always fascinating combination of documentary, epic, melodrama, and philosophical dissertation. Again, as in most of his pictures, Imamura criticizes modern civilization. He does not find the primitive life of the islanders any better but he finds it, at least, different. Also, his people often join nature at the end of his pictures (the vanished man never returns, the pornographer drifts out to sea) but here it is nature itelf that disappears, and the implication is that we are less without it. Two thirds through the film the story suddenly breaks off and a title laconically informs us that several years have passed. When the continuity is resumed everything has changed. The island has been discovered by the tourist industry. A train, taxicabs, and french fries are evident. This final sequence is extremely moving. We have come to love the primitive island and its people. Now all is changed. The cry of the Coca-Cola seller is the voice of doom.

Equally critical of modern Japan is Kaneto Shindo, whose first film, *The Story of a Beloved Wife* (Aisai Monogatari, 1951), was praised for its social criticism and damned for its sentimentality in almost equal measure, a pattern of reaction which has been maintained throughout most of the director's career. His *A Woman's Life* (Onna no Issho, 1953, based on the Maupassant novel) turned audiences against the film, rather than against the conditions which Shindo was attempting to criticize. It was not until he made *Children of the Atom Bomb* (Genbaku no Ko, 1953) that he found a subject large enough to contain a truly excessive sentimentality, and not until *Gutter* (Dobu, 1954) that his criticism of contemporary Japan became subtle enough to be effective.

Shindo was long known as a better screenwriter than a director, and it was only later, after the enthusiastic foreign reception of *The Island* (Hadaka no Shima, 1960), that his directorial reputation began. This beautiful film, constructed entirely without dialogue, remains his best. In it a truly compassionate attitude toward the hard-working people of the Inland Sea and an indignation at the social conditions which make such hard work necessary are almost perfectly balanced. There is none of the shrill political name-calling seen in *Lucky Dragon No. 5* (Daigo Fukuryo-Maru, 1958) and none of the wallowing in sentimental melodrama characteristic of *A Human Being* (Ningen, 1962).

At their finest, these earlier pictures are often remarkably concise re-creations of reality. One remembers Shindo's showing us the last minute in the life of the city of Hiroshima: a montage with a child crawling across the floor, a woman working, and a man on a streetcar, as the clock moves slowly toward the moment of explosion. One recalls the beautifully contained realism of *The Island*, with its endless vistas and always, in some corner of the screen, the family working, rowing to the mainland, or burning its dead.

At their worst the films make one wonder how much is true social criticism and how much is political propaganda. As with Hideo Sekigawa, Satsuo Yamamoto, Fumio Kamei, during this period, the party line is never completely invisible and any audience naturally feels manipulated when the purpose of the director becomes this noticeable. All of these filmmakers, however, changed direction later in their career. Shindo's change was, perhaps, the most spectacular.

Onibaba (1963) marked the beginning of the change. The director's first period film was about two women (Nobuko Otawa, who has appeared in most of Shindo's pictures since 1953, and Jitsuko Yoshimura) who live in the reed fields and prey on samurai. This is a theme to which the director returned in the much less successful *Kuroneko* (Yabu no Naka no Kuroneko, 1968). Filled with the sound of wind-whipped reeds, and with views of the sunlit swamps, it was also full of something quite alien to Shindo's earlier pictures—sex.

That sex and politics are bedfellows is not a new observation, but given the formerly almost suspiciously pure pictures of Shindo the reevaluation came with a certain suddenness. Yet, the same shift is to be observed in the films of many a leftist director. It certainly occurs in the pictures of at least several East European directors and was truly spectacular in the case of Hideo Sekigawa, the man who made the most violent of leftist-cause films and now makes such sex-filled pictures as *Iro, Himo,* and *Dani* (1965).

Whatever the reason, Shindo shortly came to interest himself almost exclusively in the subject. *Lost Sex* (Honno, 1966), *The Origin of Sex* (Sei no Kigen, 1967), *Kagero* (1969), and *Naked Nineteen-Year-Olds* (Hadaka no Jukyusai, 1970) are about such subjects as old people having intercourse, sex murders, and impotence. (A final political indication is to be descried in the latter subject: the man lost his potency after being exposed to the atom bomb.) At the same time, however, he was making such unsuccessful historical excursions as *Akuto* (1965) and such successful and disarmingly lighthearted comedies as *Tsuyomushi Onna to Yowamushi Otoko* (1968), to which the releasing company gave the misleading title *Operation Negligée*).

Though wholesale (and hence ineffectual) social criticism continues in films such as Kei Kumagai's *The Japanese Islands* (Nippon Retto, 1965), in which America and Americanized Japanese are responsible for absolutely everything that is wrong, it is plainly sex which has, for the time being, prevailed.

The Japanese, who have a category for everything, call such sex films *erodakushun,* a portmanteau word derived from "erotic productions," and, though these do not include such "quality" productions as those of Sekigawa and Shindo, they make up in numbers what they lack in everything else. Indeed, during the last several years almost half of the annual film production figure released in Japan has been composed of these hour-long *erodakushun.* Usually arranged into a triple bill, the films play in their own theaters, which never show anything else, and one of the rules of their construction is that a stimulating scene should occur every five minutes. Next to the monster films they are most rigidly constructed, but they yield to none in sheer torpor.

The trend began with the work of Tetsuji Takechi whose *Daydream* (Hakujitsumu, 1964), a simple exploitation film filled with rising breasts and clashing thighs, aroused some public dismay, including a protest from the Japanese Dentists' Association since the crazed villain who has his will with the ample heroine is a dental surgeon. Later Takechi got into deeper trouble with *Black Snow* (Kuroi Yuki, 1965). This picture, about an impotent young man who makes love—literally—with a loaded pistol, was also designed to have redeeming social content. It was highly critical of that safe target, American bases in Japan, and was loud in its protest against capitalistic Japanese—perhaps thus indicating that the politics-sex equation may also be read backwards.

Whatever redeeming content this film contained, however, it was not judged sufficient. Takeshi was sued by the Metropolitan Police Board and though he won his case and a higher court upheld the verdict, he also thereafter confined himself to sexing-up film versions of Chinese classics and the more erotic pages of *A Tale of Genji*.

This legal reversal opened the door to the *erodakushun*, though not, it is true, very far. The films are not so explicit as those to be seen in America, or in Denmark and Sweden. Also, they are more concerned with sado-masochism than with eroticism, such being the taste of their audience or (more likely) their producers. Much more eroticism is found in the ordinary Japanese picture —in films such as *Crazed Fruit, Onibaba,* and *The Affair* (Joen, 1967).

This latter picture, directed by Yoshishige Yoshida, is about a young woman (played by the director's wife, Mariko Okada) who fights against her own sensual nature. She has reason—having had a mother who sleeps around so much that she has come to react strongly against such a life. Nonetheless, when she falls—with a passing young day-laborer who had also known her mother—she falls thoroughly. The combination of a well-to-do young lady and common laborer predicates society's disapproval. Thus, the largely meaningless and certainly commonplace prejudices of society are the only normality to which she can cling.

Beautifully shot, with some formality and much economy, the film ends honestly and indecisively. Having settled with a proper man, she is waiting for a train. Suddenly, and with a surge of emotion which Yoshida makes us feel, she sees the young laborer on the other side of the tracks, waiting for a train going in the opposite direction. His train arrives first. She waits. When the train pulls clear he is gone. She continues to stand, looking. We are left to infer that at this moment she first realizes how false to her own nature she has been.

Later films of Yoshida have included the three-hour *Eros plus Massacre* (Eros plus Gyakusatsu, 1969) and *Heroic Purgatory* (Rengoku Eroika, 1970), both of which share an increasingly experimental technique but, at the same time, a needless complexity, which gives his work a mannered preciosity.

A common pattern among directors is a notable debut followed by a period of finding one's own style through a series of minor films. It is, however, to be observed more often in Japan than in other countries. Masashige Narusawa made *The Body* (Ratai, 1962), a comedy about a young girl (Michiko Saga, daughter of Isuzu Yamada) who suddenly becomes aware of her charms and proceeds to use them in a way both charming and amoral. Yoshitaro Nomura made *Tokyo Bay* (Tokyo Wan, 1963), an excellent chase-thriller, cops and robbers in the largest city in the world. Kazuo Kuroki made the beautiful if mysterious *Silence Has No Wings* (Tobenai Chimoku, 1967), and the intriguing if inconclusive *Evil Spirits of Japan* (Nihon no Akuryo, 1970). Early in his career, Hiromichi Horikawa, Kurosawa's only "pupil," made the psychological thriller *The Lost Alibi* (Kuroi Gashu, 1960). Koreyoshi Kurahara made *Black Sun* (Kuroi Taiyo, 1964), about the bond between a Japanese jazz-loving youth and an AWOL black GI. Kihachi Okamoto made the satirical comedy *Age of Assassins* (Satsujinkyo Jidai, 1966) and then went on to make such ordinary period films as *Kill* (Kiru, 1967–68) and such unexceptional war films as *Human Bullet* (Nikudan, 1968).

Notable new directors, making promising debuts, are: Koto Mori with *The River: Poem of Love* (Kawa Sono Onogiri ga Omoku, 1967), a disillusioned documentary-like film about Hiroshima, showing the city as having completely forgotten about its martyrdom; Toshio Fujito with *Cry for Dawn* (Shinobe no Sakibi, 1967), about young people and their new problems; the very far-left Shinsuke Ogawa with his *Sea of Youth* (Seinen no Umi, 1966) and his later documentaries; Morisaki Azuma with *Woman Can't Be Beaten* (Onna was Dokyo, 1969); Kiyoshi Nishimura's *Too Early to Die* (Shinu ni wa Mada Haiyai, 1969), also about today's youth; Toshio Matsumoto's *Funeral of Roses* (Bara no Soretsu, 1969), about another kind of youth—the male prostitutes, homosexuals, and transvestites of Tokyo, a film followed by his first *jidai-geki*, *Hell* (Shura, 1971); Yusuke Okada with *Akazukin* (1970), about a disaffiliated student in a disaffiliated world; and Akio Jissoji, whose *This Transient Life* (Mujo, 1970), a film about a brother and sister in love with each other, was followed by the somewhat similar *Mandala* (Mandara, 1971).

Much rarer—in all countries—are those directors who, from their first picture, clearly know what they are doing and, film by film, proceed to create an increasingly personal body of work. Among the younger directors who have in the last decade achieved this eminence is Masahiro Shinoda, who, after a period of apprenticeship turning out comedies, made *Pale Flower* (Kawaita Hanna, 1964).

In this allegory, disguised as a crime melodrama, Shinoda stated all of those themes that were to become major to his work. A gambler (Ryo Ikebe) attempts to escape from the authorities (the police on one hand, his own destiny on the other) and in the protracted chase that ensues he is at first aided but eventually betrayed by his love for an enigmatic young lady (Mariko Kaga). At the last moment, he is able to see the pattern of his life and where he has been led by it.

This theme of the frailty of love was later to become the basis of several of his pictures. *With Beauty and Sorrow* (Utsukushisha to Kanashimi to, 1965), based on a Kawabata story, was about the love of an older married woman (Kaoru Yachigusa) for a young student (Mariko Kuga again) who, perhaps innocently but certainly thoroughly, disrupts both her own life and that of her mistress. In the end the young son, who also loved the girl, is dead and she is left alone, perhaps never knowing the destruction which love for her caused. The same theme somewhat more convincingly appears in *Clouds at Sunset* (Akanegumo, 1967). Set in 1937, it is about a woman (Shinoda's wife, Shima Iwashita) who falls in love with a man (Tsutomu Yamazaki) she does not know is an army deserter. He, cynical and desperate, turns her over to another man and the loving woman agrees. At the end he is caught and realizes that he loved her. She is left behind with the knowledge of just how much love means in this world.

The stories of both films are serviceable enough in their grand and Shimpa-like ways, but the memorable thing about both is their atmosphere and the way in which Shinoda creates it. The still and claustrophobic world of the early film (Kyoto, that most closed and inbred of all Japanese cities) is captured in shot after shot of the narrow interiors of the Japanese house, walls threatening to close in, doors always shutting in one's face, and by the many scenes in graveyards (with which Kyoto abounds), the tombs standing like so many teeth, foreshortened into a forest of stone. In the latter picture, with just a few details, Shinoda rigorously creates the whole world of 1937, its frivolity, its uneasiness; the tawdry summer gaiety of a provincial hot-spring resort; that vague sense of foreboding, that undefined pathos which recall Chekhov and Ibsen. Shinoda does this in a number of ways, but mainly through selection of detail (light on tile roofs, the single rising-sun flag, the sound of cicadas, the way a girl puts up her hair), an apt use of camera movement (a slow pan can mean resignation, a backward dolly can indicate or deepen tragedy), and an extraordinary sound track (a number of tiny, meaningful sounds: distant trains, a faraway dog, the small noise of a match being struck). In this ability to create atmosphere Shinoda is in a direct line from Mizoguchi.

He also resembles Mizoguchi in his very Japanese concept of destiny. It is there, as palpable for the Japanese directors as it was for Thomas Hardy, and there is equally no escaping it. In *Double Suicide* (Shinju Ten no Amijima, 1969) Shinoda can film a Chikamatsu play with almost no changes (as could Mizoguchi in his *A Story from Chikamatsu*) because both directors and the playwright share this fatalistic concept of waiting destiny, and the inability of any man to escape it.

In the 1969 film, which is based on one of Chikamatsu's plays for the Bunraku (the Osaka puppet theater), Shinoda takes brilliant advantage of the dolls to create the feeling of humans helplessly controlled. The film opens in the Osaka Bunraku theater itself and all of the preparations for making the film are seen: light cables are laid, camera positions are determined, Shinoda himself appears, as do his technicians. The story itself begins as a documentary on the doll drama, each doll being held and manipulated by the three men, two of them masked, who perform traditionally. As the story proceeds, however, the director substitutes his actors, and the puppeteers no longer directly control them. Yet, they remain; they are always there, in every scene, masked by black gauze behind which we see their faces, compassionate yet helpless as they watch the characters (now thoroughly human) thread the labyrinth to their doom.

The story is a simple one, the conflict of love versus duty (the almost invariable plot of Japanese classical drama), with the young lovers caught between the two demands. Shinoda, however, has given it far greater depth by allowing no escape, and by insisting upon the objective, the dispassionate. He later turned to Kabuki in *The Scandalous Adventures of Buraikan* (Buraikan, 1970), a picaresque adventure film based on a later (1881) play about the last decadent days of the Tokugawa period. Here love has become a frivolous affectation and destiny the grand debacle at the end of the picture which engulfs the entire cast.

Shinoda's old Edo no more existed than did Federico Fellini's ancient Rome but, like it, becomes both believable and memorable through the director's consciously creating an entire and much heightened world. The manner is broadly theatrical, and at times the language is as mandarin as the acting is Byzantine. Completely artificial, this world prevails and becomes believable through the sheer mass of detail which Shinoda (like Fellini) lavishes on his historical extravaganza. A bunch of rogues decide they have had enough of repressive feudal ways, so they join the common people and revolt. They lose and are this time completely repressed. The theme is so contemporary as to be almost allegorical of the demonstrations and student riots which Shinoda was also thinking of. Here artificiality—a quality which has marred some of the director's work—is a part of the style. The world itself has become artificial, and we see it through a controlled style which is completely formalized. The hieratic gestures and heightened language create an atmosphere (and hence a reality) which is dazzling and—because we know that the world is not, after all, like this—oddly moving.

Kinoshita's use of Kabuki in *The Ballad of Narayama* failed to move audiences, because the director was insisting upon naturalistic detail in a theatrical and unnatural situation. Shinoda's use of Kabuki in this film is very moving because he heightens the artificiality of the already artificial. Consequently we must bring all of our understanding and compassion to the picture. Shinoda's coldness, his apparent refusal to do more than show, his apparent disinclination to tell one how to feel, is a part of his concern for disclosing the pattern of the men's lives, for his insistence upon the implacability of fate.

In *Punishment Island* (Shokei no Shima, 1966) the pattern is particularly interesting. A young man (Akira Nitta) returns to the island where he spent his orphaned youth. There he was (along with all the other boys) tortured by the man (Rentaro Mikuni) whom he later discovers was also the military policeman who killed his parents. When the young man finally tracks down the older, he is horrified to discover that the old man now remembers nothing at all of what he did to the boy. Faced not with rage or fear, but something much worse—the indifference of time itself—the young man completes his lifelong plan and punishes the old man. This completed, he races down the mountain, gets on a boat, and the film suddenly ends. The last image is the young man turning away with excitement and satisfaction from the island where until now he has spiritually continued to live. The film asks that most important question at its very end: What will he do now? The full horror comes into view as the house lights go up. The real cruelty is that the man has devoted his life to revenge, and so has wasted, not just his youth, but his entire life. This upsetting conclusion turns morality upside down. It seems to indicate that the victim has no hope for redress, that revenge cannot but be hollow, that evil remains evil because all of this is so. It is not that turning the other cheek is a virtue;

it is simply all that a human being can do. The picture is disguised as a melodrama, in that it appears to be about that favorite film subject, revenge. At the same time it is multilayered and rich in its implications. One may read it, just as well, as an allegory or—and this is the level which reaches the emotions—a mysterious and disturbing parable.

The same theme appears in *Silence* (Chimoku, 1971), based on the Shusaku Endo novel, about two Portuguese padres who come to Japan during the sixteenth century. It is not revenge that keeps them alive but faith. At the end, one of them comes to realize that faith—or any single idea—is not enough for a lifetime. He recants in order to save some peasants from torture. His life now completely empty, he continues to live, and is given a Japanese name, a Japanese house, a Japanese wife.

Our destiny will catch us at the end and love, that supposed lifesaver, sinks before anything else. Yet, in the end, it is the pattern of one's life which is interesting and meaningful. This is the theme that all Shinoda films have in common, which is seen in such a routine period picture as *Sarutobi* (Ibun Sarutobi Sasuke, 1965), and which is the basis of one of the director's best films, *Assassination* (Ansatsu, 1964).

This picture takes place in 1863 (with flashbacks to earlier times) and deals with the plots and counterplots which resulted in the opening of the country. Shinoda, like most period film directors, takes for granted that the audience knows the ramifications of the story. Unlike most, however, he quickly draws the viewer into these complications whether he truly understands them or not. The reason is that Shinoda is not interested in the intricacies of history. They are useful only in establishing various kinds of action necessary for the disclosure of his main concern. This is the shapes or patterns of men's lives. And this interest accounts both for his cursory treatment of history and for the structure of the film itself.

In the first reel we believe we are being introduced to the heroes and that they are talking about the villains. By the time the second reel is over, however, we have heard enough to know that the first men might be villains and that the "villains" may well be heroic. As the film progresses, we are led to question the ethical motives of everyone in the film. The screenplay, which Shinoda helped write, as he does for all his films, uses the methods of Orson Welles's *Citizen Kane* or, perhaps better, Francesco Rosi's *Salvatore Giuliano.* The film loops back again and again into the main character's life, never solving any of the problems, nor resolving any of the differences. As a consequence, the character (played by Tetsuro Tamba) becomes more and more alive throughout the course of the film. In this sense, a very complicated plot becomes simple as the director makes one live through it.

Shinoda's Shogunate Japan—seen here in *Double Suicide,* in *Sarutobi,* in *Buraikan,* and in *Silence*—is a world in itself. Again one thinks of Mizoguchi, because there has been no other director since him who could create the feeling of historical locale as well. In *Assassination* Shinoda creates a real world (much of which is shot in actual eighteenth-century buildings), one which his characters may naturally and convincingly inhabit. Shinoda is not interested in the Mizoguchi ethos, however; he does not attempt (nor is he interested in attempting) that bittersweet reconciliation between duty and inclination which is the message of Mizoguchi. The younger director is interested in the patterns of men's lives and in the character of a man free enough and hopelessly doomed enough to be nihilistic in a rigidly repressive and obsessively codified world.

Thus Shinoda, to a degree, shares an interest with both Ichikawa and Kurosawa, both of whom show us a freedom of action which is often, though not invariably, foiled by fate. A belief this strong and this consistent results in a personal style of considerable strength.

As a stylist Kon Ichikawa is one of Japan's most brilliant. Though he had been making films for many years, he first came into prominence with *The Harp of Burma* (Biruma no Tategoto, 1956), a picture about a young soldier who decides to stay behind, to become a monk and to bury the dead, and one which, despite some crude editing—not by the director—managed to generate considerable power. His first popular success was *Punishment Room* (Shokei no Heya), a curious but rather routine juvenile delinquency film, which was followed by *The Men of Tohoku* (Tohoku no Zumutachi, 1957), a half-documentary, half-expressionist comedy. In the latter film meticulously realistic—and often real—sets were combined with painted perspectives and frankly artificial decor.

Ichikawa's mature style did not become evident, however, until *Conflagration* (Enjo, 1958), also known as *Flame of Torment,* the screen version of the novel by Yukio Mishima, translated as *The Temple of the Golden Pavilion,* about the acolyte who deliberately set fire to and destroyed Kyoto's famous Kinkakuji. The visuals of the film are superb. Ichikawa and Kazuo Miyagawa, the cameraman for *Rashomon* and *Yojimbo,* used the widescreen in an intelligent and creative manner, and the textures captured in black and white were—even for Japan—beyond comparison. Particularly impressive was the use of architecture. Ichikawa (and Miyagawa, who is fond of using only a portion of the widescreen) would situate their action at the far left, for example, balancing it with architectural detail which, as one scene followed the other, perfectly re-created the temple atmosphere. For one short scene Ichikawa set his student high on the balcony of the superb Kiyomizudera in Kyoto, then shot from the valley far below with a telephoto lens. The result is a dazzling bas-relief of foreshortened temple roof, the student tiny and black and lost amid the gray maze of tiles and weathered wood. Yet such setups always serve primarily to emphasize the meaning of the scene, in this case the boy's first awareness of his isolation and loneliness. Though aesthetically prodigal, the film never exploited aestheticism for its own sake. Likewise, a richness of psychological detail was used for the sole end of telling a story. We are told, through dialogue and through controlled and utterly unobstrusive flashbacks, the story of this boy who eventually comes to feel that he must destroy what he most loves—the pavilion. We are given a number of reasons: his sluttish mother, the early death of his father, the hypocrisy of the head priest, the evilness of his friend. All of this motivation, and all of the visual wealth which accompanies it, resulted in the creation of an extremely strong atmosphere, a film style which was individual and at the same time fitting.

Just as beautiful and just as disturbing was *The Key* (Kagi, 1959), known abroad as both *Odd Obsession* and *Strange Obsession.* If *Conflagration* equated beauty and love with destruction, *The Key* equated them with illness and death. The film, based rather loosely on Junichiro Tanizaki's best-selling novel of the same name, examines the love life of a middle-aged Kyoto couple—Ganjiro Nakamura and Machiko Kyo—and parallels this with the affair of their daughter and her young doctor fiancé. The picture, like the novel, is not particularly interested in romantic liaisons, however, and sacrifices any melodramatic possibilities by making each member of the quartet perfectly aware of what the others are doing. Thus the husband knows about, indeed encourages, the fact that the young doctor and his wife are enjoying a kind of affair; the doctor knows all about the highly irregular love life of the married couple; and the couple themselves are quite aware of what the youngsters are about. Not only is there listening at keyholes and peeping through *shoji* but the husband also takes pictures of his wife and then passes them on to the doctor to develop, he in turn showing them to the daughter.

Eroticism is omnipresent, though not the scented variety of, say, *Les Amants*. Rather, the screen is cluttered with hypodermic needles, catheters, unmade beds—all filmed by Miyagawa in muted color. Erotic obsession is presented with such near-claustrophobic intensity that one longs for outdoor scenes, anything to get away from that dark and keyholed and magnificently photographed house. Yet this quality accounts for the power of this very powerful film: the spectator is made a participant. Although all the principals know at least as much as the viewer, nothing is ever discussed, nothing is brought into the open. Rather, everything is hidden, secreted away. The film becomes remarkably suggestive, as one double meaning follows another. There is an extraordinary scene in which the husband is making love to his wife. For one shocked instant we think we are witnessing his orgasm. Then we realize—with equal shock—that he has had a stroke. From then on he is paralyzed, unable to move or talk, while the members of his family cavort in front of him. Yet, despite all this, *The Key* is never meretricious. Unlike other efforts—Japanese and foreign—titillation is not the ultimate intention. Ichikawa is telling us something unpleasant, certainly, but nonetheless true. It is a new interpretation of the love-death theme, in which some of the most sordid of human actions are captured by means of the sheerest physical beauty.

Fires on the Plain (Nobi, 1959) is taken from the war novel by Shohei Oka and is frankly concerned with death and with that last refuge of desire—cannibalism. Very little was left out of the book and what the film contributed was a superb visualization, a studied and controlled visual style (fully half of the film had no dialogue whatever) which—like all strong styles—created a world of its own, one which forced our sympathies, commanded empathy, and eventually enmeshed our emotions.

One remembers: the private—played by Eiji Funakoshi—in the deserted village, coming upon the mound of dead Japanese soldiers; the slow march through the forest, a plane approaches, all fall to the ground, the plane passes, only half the men rise to stagger on and not one looks back; the shot of a man tasting salt for the first time in months, an involuntary tear running down his cheek; an encounter with a dying soldier on a mountain top, the soldier eating the earth he has himself soiled; the long marches in the rain, when the shoes discarded by one soldier are retrieved by another whose own are even worse; men dead on their haunches, like animals, with even the dignity of death taken from them. That we are not horrified, experience no revulsion, is due entirely to the simple dignity of the script (written, as are all Ichikawa's scripts, with his wife), to the director's honesty, and to the sometimes appalling beauty of the images.

Ichikawa's section of the three-part *A Woman's Testament* began in the manner of experimental cinema and ended in the broadest farce. A young man finds a mysterious woman on the beach. He finds her, one might add, amid a very amusing collection of *avant-garde* film clichés. She takes him back to the mysterious house in which she lives, but it turns out that she is a complete impostor. He, quicker than she, finds out first and there is a final discovery scene where the cheated cheats the cheater.

The director's most popular film has been *Younger Brother* (Ototo, 1960), called *Little Brother* at showings at the 1961 Cannes Festival, in which an elder sister, Keiko Kishi, watches a younger brother, Hiroshi Kawaguchi, to whom she is very attached, die of tuberculosis. Again marvelously photographed by Miyagawa, the film—unusual for an Ichikawa picture—tacitly championed the Japanese family system and found praiseworthy the sister's devotion to her brother over all other males. Like Toyoda's *Grass Whistle* it was about an adolescent accepting an adult situation in an adult manner, but Ichikawa is here on the side of the adults. Unlike the Toyoda film and, let us say, a picture like the Melville-Cocteau *Les Enfants Terribles,* also about an abnormally close brother-sister relationship, *Younger Brother* firmly approves such closely knit family ties.

Almost completely opposite was the excellent *Bonchi* (1960—the title, untranslatable, is an Osaka dialect word, used to affectionately designate the eldest son), a film in which the devastating honesty of the script was matched by the extraordinary beauty of the presentation. The traditional family system has probably never been more brutally presented, nor the people involved shown with more candor and understanding.

The women who run this particular family (and one

of the points of the film is that the family, or at least this well-to-do Osaka prewar family, is controlled by women, by a mother and daughter—beautifully played by Kikue Mori and Isuzu Yamada) are the very ones who create the situations against which the women in the Naruse films are attempting, unsuccessfully, to escape.

The problem is that the grandmother—not a comic dragon in the Kinoshita manner but a rocklike and rather frightening person—has decided that the family needs an heir and this means that the son—the late Raizo Ichikawa, who also played the student in *Conflagration* —must marry and produce. What they want is a girl, so that they can later adopt a husband—just as the boy's own father was adopted—and thus keep the power among the women.

His first child is a boy and the furious grandmother sends the new wife back home. From then on the two women encourage the completely spoiled boy—a character somewhat like the hero in Toyoda's *Marital Relations* —to have as many girls as he wants. But it all comes to nothing. As in *Ten Dark Women* (Kuroi Junin no Onna, 1961) matriarchy, sterile in essence, defeats itself. The grandmother commits suicide. All of the women in the hero's life—and there are a great many—drift out of it. At the end of the film, as at the beginning, he is seen as an old man, gossiping with a crony—Ganjiro Nakamura, the head priest in *Conflagration*—about all the women in his life, strangely untouched by time itself, as though the matriarchy were, in some strange way, still living on in him.

The picture is a panorama of a certain kind of Japanese society, a microcosm of what is most Japanese about traditional living. We are shown this with an honesty that is ruthless, and, at the same time, with a beauty that refines and transfigures everything it touches. In this film, as in their others, Ichikawa and Miyagawa insist that corruption and beauty are no strangers. This is the theme of both *Conflagration* and *The Key*. Thus, in *Bonchi* we find this cruel matriarchal story, this slaughtering of all the innocents, told in terms of the most transcendent beauty. Time and again Miyagawa's superlative photography redeems the most sordid objects and actions, seeming to insist that there is beauty everywhere. In the same way, the director insists that even in the middle of the most ferocious of machinations there is goodness. A charming scene is where grandmother and mother, like two little girls, are sitting before the traditional doll exhibition on Girls' Day, for the instant as innocent as the girl children they are thinking of and half-pretending to be. The father's deathbed scene, filled as it is with the barbarity of his having to feel it necessary to apologize for dying, is redeemed by the exquisite dignity of his manner. The quite monstrousness of the scene where the grandmother, to prove that she has the kind of skin seen only in women who bear children, bares her breast to her daughter, is redeemed by the director's allowing us to understand that in a woman who has really little else, this is, perhaps, a legitimate pride. The family meeting scene, in which it is decided that the wife is to be sent home, is so quietly beautiful that one almost forgives the people their wretched self-interest. It is a long, immaculately lit, single scene, five people talking in the late summer afternoon, one of the many subtleties of which is that it is so composed that each of the people commands equal attention, while the scene itself is of such a loveliness that one could look at it twice as long and not get tired of it.

Again, in *The Sin* (Hakai, 1961), also known as *The Outcast,* a brooding and brutal film about the discrimination directed against the outcast class, the *burakumin,* Ichikawa alternates scenes as black as they are bleak against scenes of a supernal beauty. The young school teacher (Raizo Ichikawa) who "confesses" that he is of the pariah caste to his room full of young pupils—a very painful sequence—must now leave the small mountain community. He is met by the maid, the only one who cared for him. They say good-bye. Suddenly it begins to snow. The camera turns to catch this mantle of white covering up the black mountains, black forests. It is a beautiful moment because it is a metaphor for the entire film. The young teacher will always begin over again; white will always cover black.

Ichikawa waited for weeks in his expensive mountain location for that snowfall and though some directors—Kurosawa, Mizoguchi, Ozu, among them—have gotten away with spending that much of the company's money for a reason that all film companies everywhere would regard as needless, Ichikawa's company, dissatisfied with such masterpieces as *Enjo* and *Bonchi*, decided, first, to keep tighter reign on their best director and, eventually, to dismiss him. Thus Ichikawa, though returning to feature production with *Pourquoi?* (Ai Futatabi, 1971), for a time joined the ranks of those others—Nakahira, Masamura, Kawabe—whose careers have been circumscribed if not stopped by the companies for which they worked.

After the dark honesty of *The Sin*, Ichikawa was told to make the sunny, happy, family film, *I Am Two* (Watashi wa Nisai, 1962), about a baby and his parents. As further punishment he was to make *Money Talks* (Zeni no Odori, 1964), an ordinary cops-and-robbers script starring the company's biggest moneymaker (and a good actor besides), Shintaro Katsu. He was also—and it must have seemed at the time almost a calculated insult—to remake that old tearjerker, *The Revenge of Yukinojo* (Yukinojo Hengi, 1963), also known as *An Actor's Revenge*.

Ichikawa triumphed over all three assignments. Once, when asked the greatest influence on his work, he answered, honestly and without hesitation, that it was Walt Disney. And it is true that his first picture was the puppet film *Musume Dojoji* (1946—never released because the Allied Occupation was suspicious of anything traditional and the picture was based on the Kabuki dance). Indeed, he later became so interested in the Italian mouse puppet, Topo Gigio, that he made the entirely disastrous *Topo Gigio and the Missile War* (Top Gigio no Botan Senso, 1967). Still later he created for the Sumitomo Pavilion the enchanting combination of film and marionettes which so delighted thousands at the Osaka 1970 Exposition.

In *I am Two* he dispensed with the parents at once and shot the entire film through the wondering eyes of a baby, including a little cartoon sequence as an *hommage à Disney*. *Money Talks* was done in the style of a newspaper cartoon strip, with outrageous dialogue and even more outrageous acting. And in *The Revenge of Yukinojo* he triumphed over his material so completely that the result is something of a masterpiece—though just what kind is difficult to say.

The tired melodrama upon which this film was based, old-fashioned when it originally appeared back in the twenties, was, of course, just the film for Ichikawa not to do—it was like asking Buñuel to remake *Stella Dallas*. Nonetheless, the director saw possibilities in it. He and his wife, Natto Wada, examined the creaking scenario (upon which Daisuke Ito and Teinosuke Kinugasa, among others, had worked decades before) and found it so bad as to be good. In casting, he therefore insisted upon Kazuo Hasegawa, in films almost from their inception, an aging but still popular matinee idol, and a talented if occasionally overemotional actor. Then Ichikawa set out, as he said, "to see what the movies can do."

He produced, among other things, a tour-de-force, willfully scrambled stage and screen, tried every color experiment he could think of, and created one of the most visually entertaining films ever to come from Japan. At the same time, however, being Ichikawa, he made a very disturbing picture. The love scenes—with the aging but dignified Hasegawa playing a man playing a woman to the young Ayako Wakao—are both arresting and troubling. An innuendo, always to be inferred, gives all of these scenes an ambivalent edge which, intended or not, makes them fairly unforgettable. Finally, with the spirit of camp never far away, never being certain whether Hasegawa is being made a fool of or is giving a great performance which the director is merely recording, one begins to feel little by little the pathos and terror which must always have lurked in this hackneyed little story.

Though Disney would not, perhaps, have appreciated the nature of the tribute, he might have admired the sheer amount of presentation in it. Though no showman, in the pejorative sense of the word, Ichikawa in his earliest and in his latest films displays a cinematic flair which suits equally such early comedies as *Mr. Pu* (Pu-san, 1953), based on a popular newspaper cartoon series, *The Billionaire* (Okumanchoja, 1954), and the later *Alone on the Pacific* (Taiheiyo no Hitoribochi, 1964), as well as the series of documentaries he has made since leaving his company.

The finest of these is *Tokyo Olympiad* (1965), a full documentary of the 1964 Olympic Games in Tokyo. If Leni Riefenstahl attempted, successfully, to aggrandize the games, then Ichikawa attempted, equally successfully, to humanize them. Time and again, Ichikawa's camera turns away from the major events to capture details of the spectators, to watch the athletes at rest, to celebrate those who came in, not first, but third, or last. One remembers the incisive use of slow motion during the one-hundred-yard dash, the beautiful repeated shots in the pole-vaulting competition, the use of telephoto lenses to give impact and immediacy during the shot-put event, and the long, brilliant climax of the marathon. But one remembers equally that long and beautiful final shot (seen only in one of the several versions): the celebrations are over, the stadium is empty; a man with a ladder crosses the field, far away; from even farther away comes the sound of children at play. The games were, after all, only games; they are over, and life goes on.

The original, and finest, of all the various versions of this picture was seen only once. The Olympic Organizing Board did not like the film. Or rather, like all boards, it was undecided until one of its members, a well-known politician, Ichiro Kono, now dead, spoke against it, his reason being that he had presumably wanted something like the Riefenstahl film, more sports and less people. He was important enough that the board went to his side and re-editing was demanded. The result of this was the version of the picture that played in Japan. Much of what is best in the film is missing, as well as the memorable final scene and all of the marvelously photographed cross-country run.

When Ichikawa came to make the international version of the picture, however, he was able again to insert much of what he had been forced to remove. Back went all of the various crowd details, scenes of the athletes at rest and at play, and the memorable final shot. Cut out, however, for reasons of length, were the cross-country run, the splendid water polo sections, and many of the main track events.

This remains the best version of the film and it has been seen (with minor deletion or additions) in most countries of the world with the exception of America, where it was bought by a small sports-oriented film company, which butchered the picture and put in the type of Clem McCarthy narration that Ichikawa had taken such pains to avoid. Later much of the footage that Ichikawa had himself rejected was cemented together by anonymous hands and the result was the very dull *Inspiration of the Century* (Seido no Kando, 1966), which did, by accident as it were, include some sections of the original picture—the cross-country run, for example —which Ichikawa had himself been forced to cut out.

That the film remains magnificent (the international edition at any rate) despite what has been done to it, is an indication of Ichikawa's humanity as much as it is of his undoubted cinematic flair. Its success, which was enormous, both in Japan and abroad, however, resulted in Ichikawa's suddenly being type-cast (so far as production companies went) as a maker of "official" documentaries.

He was asked, for example, to do a film on little-league baseball, which resulted in *Youth* (Seishun, 1968). To ask the director of *Enjo* and *Bonchi* to do a sandlot-baseball film is, in one sense, absurd. In another sense, however, it obviously fit the director, because the finished film is among his most moving. He begins the film in the winter in the far north of Japan and beautifully and movingly photographs the youngsters as they prepare for the spring games. So right is this preparation, and so loving is Ichikawa's regard that the spring season becomes almost as thrilling as anything in *Tokyo Olympiad.* This film is filled with the care and craft that distinguish all of his later pictures and in it he proved again his extraordinary ability to surmount all problems by simply treating the problem at hand as though its inception had generated within himself.

This is certainly true of two later commissioned films, one very small and the other very large. *Kyoto* (1969) is a beautiful half-hour film commissioned by a foreign typewriter company which returns us (this time in color) to the world of *Enjo.* Ichikawa's Kyoto is one of stillness and repose, a dark and ancient capital filled with echoes and shafts of light, with ancient temples and still water.

The large film is *Japan and the Japanese* (Nihon to Nihonjin, 1970), another half-hour film but designed to be shown on the mammoth nine-panel screen of the Japanese Pavilion at the Osaka Exposition. From the first image—a terrifying aerial descent into Mount Fuji—the picture is as spectacular as anything on film. At the same time, however, Ichikawa's humor and humanism is there: a breathtakingly beautiful panorama of the Japanese Alps pans down, down, down, to reveal a colossal traffic jam; during the most exquisite of the many views of Fuji we hear a small boy complaining: "Mama, where is Fuji anyhow? I can't see it. Where is it?" The conclusion is enchanting—long, soft, and very Ichikawa-like—with the islands of Japan slowly passing before us and a great sun burning on the horizon. This is surely the most beautiful paean any filmmaker has ever given his country.

The seemingly various parts of Ichikawa come into focus when one remembers that his extremely personal style, one of the most finished in contemporary Japanese cinema, is predicated upon a kind of duality. Willing pupil of Disney, he is at the same time drawn to the dark matter of *Enjo* and *Bonchi*. Maker of official documentaries, he is also drawn to the most intimate of psychological revelations. A humanist, he is, almost consequently, drawn to death and destruction. All of this is somehow redeemed through beauty.

In this, Ichikawa is very like Mizoguchi, whose finest films gain much of their power from his resolving the conflict between the ugliness of much of his subject matter—the crucified lovers, the lives of prostitutes, women sold into slavery—and the extraordinary beauty with which it is shown. Ichikawa has been criticized as being an aesthete—by those who prefer the much rougher statements of an Imai or a Kobayashi—but this very interest in aesthetics is, after all, just what accounts for the extreme power of a Mizoguchi or an Ichikawa film. The latter's condemnation of the traditional is much more finished and much more subtle than that of Imai but it is just as strong. What he occasionally lacks, perhaps, is directness, oddly, that very feeling for realism which is the strongest attribute of the cinema. One sometimes feels that Ichikawa's films have been worked on and worked over so long, are so artfully constructed, so subtly arranged, that one appreciates but does not quite believe. If they lack anything, it is immediacy; just as the films of Imai and Kobayashi, Oshima and Masumura, lack that interest in character delineation, in the intricate interplay of character with environment, which is so much of film style, since this is just what is sacrificed through exclusive interest in social issues.

These two qualities—an interest in film aesthetics as a medium of emotional communication and an equal interest in social issues which are larger than the single man—are reconciled in the work of Akira Kurosawa, a film director whom the last twenty-five years has revealed as so thoroughly whole and in that sense so completely great that one can compare him only to Yasujiro Ozu—his utter opposite, the director most antithetical, and yet one with whom, oddly, he shares more than any other.

Like Ozu, he is a master stylist. He adds to a given theme, or plot, or incident, all of the circumstances calculated to produce the entire effect that the theme or the plot or the incident ought to produce. He creates an entire world, along with all the laws which govern it. He shows character by presenting what motivates that character. And he suggests the environment, the context, of every action. One of the effects of this is that Kurosawa's world is a private one, one that is uniquely his own. One minute of an Ozu or a Kurosawa film is enough to let you know whose it is.

At the same time the work of Kurosawa represents a departure from the tradition of the Japanese film. He has always refused to make the expected kind of picture. He has consistently confused critics and, sometimes, audiences by his continual refusal to accept the prevailing philosophy of the Japanese film; he is firmly against tradition for its own sake. Rather, he has sought and found originality, and as a group his films constitute an imposing experimental achievement. For this reason, the Japanese often call him their "least Japanese" director and the description is apt. He is "Western" in that he is a creator, in the pioneer sense of the word. Completely uninterested in the standard program film, he has gone beyond the accepted confines of cinematic language as the Japanese understand it, and in so doing has considerably widened them.

Perhaps this was the reason that Kurosawa was the first director to be "discovered" abroad and perhaps this was why, once found, he was so quickly accepted in foreign countries. On the other hand, Kurosawa himself—tired of being called "Western" by critics both at home and abroad—has said: "I have not read one review from abroad that has not read false meanings into my pictures . . . I would never make a picture especially for foreign audiences. If a work cannot have meaning to Japanese audiences, I—as a Japanese artist—am simply not interested."

Though Kurosawa may create entirely for the Japanese audiences, he completely disapproves of what they are usually given to see. In particular he dislikes the continual emphasis that Japanese society is a sick society, though he himself does not deny this fact. He feels that one of the results of the pessimistic outlook of Japanese films is an invalidating weakness in the films' moral statement.

And if, like all great creators, Kurosawa is a moralist, then, like all stylists, he manages to hide the fact superlatively well.

The moral of the Kurosawa film seems simple—but like all moral statements, it is deceptively simple. In baldest form it is related to the "humanism" that critics, Japanese and foreign, usually refer to in discussions of Kurosawa films. In this context it means merely that Kurosawa, like most creators, likes people, believes in them, and hopes for the best—a statement which could include every other film director, good or bad. The key to Kurosawa's particular humanism, if that is even the word for it, is much less apparent.

It is Dostoevskian, just as Ozu's humanism—with its concern for the passing of time, for the restricted canvas which represents the entire world, and for the outward actions of people—might be called Tolstoy-like. The direct influence of Dostoevsky is considerable. From his youth Kurosawa felt a great affinity with the Russian author; he himself talks about reading *The Idiot* and *Crime and Punishment* over and over again. The author's thought and style had the greatest influence on his film work; he had long felt that he wanted to acknowledge this debt by doing a picture based on Dostoevsky. He produced a Japanese version of *The Idiot*, and himself calls *Drunken Angel* "a film in the Dostoevsky manner." He has said: "I know of no one so compassionate as he; this compassion is quite different from that of the ordinary person's. Ordinary people turn their eyes away from tragedy; he looks straight into it and suffers with the victims: he is more god than human."

This Dostoevskian "humanism" is seen at its best when Kurosawa allows it to dictate the basic precepts of the film, and then works through it. When he uses words like "love" and "compassion" in the dialogue the effect is trite—perhaps because his emotion, like that of Dostoevsky, must be shown rather than merely expressed.

Drunken Angel (Yoidore Tenshi, 1948)—the screenplay written by Kurosawa along with Keinosuke Uegusa—is an exercise in the Dostoevsky manner. Though the director later said that he made the film "to expose gangsters and to show how silly they are as humans" he was obviously just as concerned with the necessity of compassion, and its responsibilities. The almost existential theme is also the plot. An alcoholic doctor—played by Takashi Shimura—finds a young hoodlum—Toshiro Mifune in one of his first starring roles—who has tuberculosis and attempts to nurse him back to health. Nothing could be less outwardly tender than the reflections between the two men: the doctor is a compassionate bully, drunk most of the time, and always eminently tactless; the gangster is unsure of himself, given to braggadocio, and almost as afraid of the doctor as he is of the disease. Their snarlings, their occasional fist fights, are based upon mutual need: the doctor, a failure in the eyes of the world, insists upon saving this seemingly worthless young man; the gangster, a failure just as complete, feels that a final defeat would be salvation at the hands of this man who attracts and repels him almost equally.

Their mutual antagonism—a hidden parable on the responsibilities of compassion—is set in the ruin of postwar Japan where standards have been completely destroyed, where an entire society lies open, helpless, and festering. The doctor lives near a great crater, now filled with oil-scummed water. Every day he goes out of his way to frighten the children playing around it, to frighten them for their own good. The gangster, surrounded by others more successful than he because more brutal, is drawn by this oily sump. He may hurry past it during the day but it is here that he returns and, at the end of the film, it is fitting that, though dead, he should be there. The bar girl who loved him is carrying his ashes, neatly wrapped in white cloth, and stops by its banks to talk to the doctor, who knows he has failed but who with the almost maniacal energy of the truly compassionate at once turns his mind to other matters. In the final scene we see him hurrying along with a young girl, once tubercular, now saved. He is having a holiday from compassion. The final comment seems to be that, in a way, both he and the gangster were true to themselves to the end. Failure may be implicit but there has, at least, been a moment of comprehension.

In *Stray Dog* (Nora Inu, 1949) the Dostoevskian duality continues. In this picture a young detective, Toshiro Mifune, has his pistol stolen. Not only were pistols hard to get in 1949, but also Mifune feels that the symbol of his status, almost his only identification in a corrupt and chaotic world, has been taken from him. In a very special sense he feels unmanned. With great energy he therefore dedicates himself to the seemingly useless task of attempting to find it. His odyssey, seen by Kurosawa almost as a comic epic, carries him though all segments of Japanese society. Like the search for the bicycle in *Bicycle Thieves* it is at once comment, allegory, and adventure story. And, as in all good adventure stories, the search is rewarded, the grail is found. At the same time, the much-desired pistol is stripped of all its significance. Mifune catches the thief, chases him over a marsh, fights with him among the flowering weeds of an early spring. Finally, completely covered with mud (in a scene reminiscent of *Drunken Angel* where the gangster, just before he is killed, falls against cans of white paint which utterly transfigure him, an apotheosis before death), the two, exhausted, lie panting, side by side, and the camera, for the first time dropping the aloof, dispassionate, attitude of a documentary machine, peers curiously at them through the blossoms of spring—and finds them identical. In a sequence much similar to that, in the later *High and Low* (Tengoku to Jigoku, 1963), the plate of glass separating kidnaper and victim in prison reflects and fuses their reflected faces, so that we cannot tell the two apart. Muddy and unrecognizable, lying side by side, cop and robber are one and the same. The disputed pistol lies disregarded between them, now finally meaningless.

In *Scandal* (Shubun, 1950), a complete lack of compassion is responsible for the difficulties of a young artist (Toshiro Mifune) and a famous singing star (Yoshiko Yamaguchi) whose friendship is completely misunder-

Children Hand in Hand, 1962. Directed by Susumu Hani.

Tokyo Bay, 1963. Directed by Yoshitaro Nomura.

An Actor's Revenge, 1963. Directed by Kon Ichikawa. Kazuo Hasegawa.

Yearning, 1963. Directed Mikio Naruse. Yuzo Kayan Hideko Takamine.

High and Low, 1963. I rected by Akira Kurosaw Toshiro Mifune, Tatsu Nakadai.

She and He, 1963. Direct by Susumu Hani. Sachi Hidari (left).

Onibaba, 1963. Directed by Kaneto Shindo. Nobuko Otowa, Jitsuko Yoshimura.

The Scent of Incense, 1964. Directed by Keisuke Kinoshita. Haruko Sugimura (left), Mariko Okada (right).

Alone on the Pacific, 1964. Directed by Kon Ichikawa. Yujiro Ishihara.

Woman in the Dunes, 1964. Directed by Hiroshi Teshigahara. Kyoko Kishida, Eiji Okada.

A Story from Echigo, 1964. Directed by Tadashi Imai. Yoshiko Sakuma, Shoichi Ozawa.

Pale Flower, 1964. Directed by Masahiro Shinoda. Ryo Ikebe (rear).

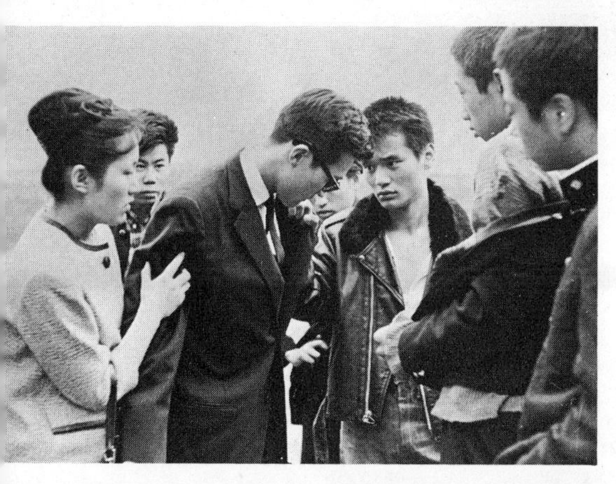

Juvenile Delinquents, 1964. Directed by Kazuo Kawabe.

Assassination, 1964. Directed by Masahiro Shinoda. Eiji Okada (left), Ko Kimura (right).

Manji, 1964. Directed by Yasuzo Masumura. Ayako Wakao, Kyoko Kishida.

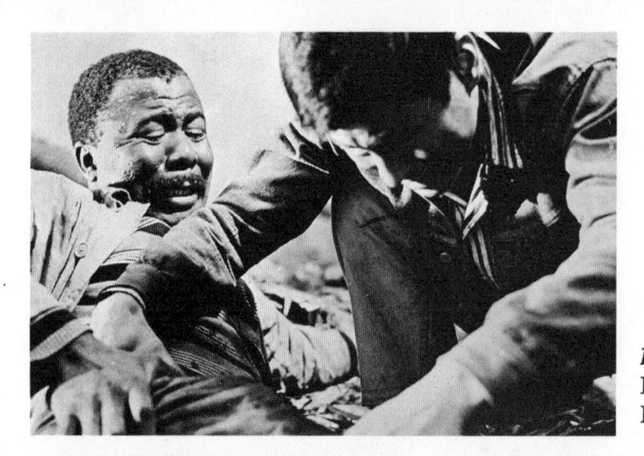

Black Sun, 1964. Directed by Koreyoshi Kurahara. Chiko Lourant, Tamio Kawaji.

The Innocent Witch, 1965. Directed by Heinosuke Gosho. Jitsuko Yoshimura.

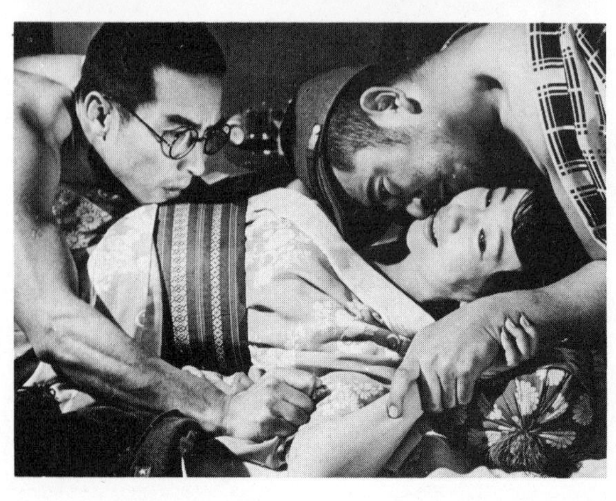

The Hoodlum Soldier, 1965. Directed by Yasuzo Masumura. Takahiro Tamura, Keiko Awaji, Shintaro Katsu.

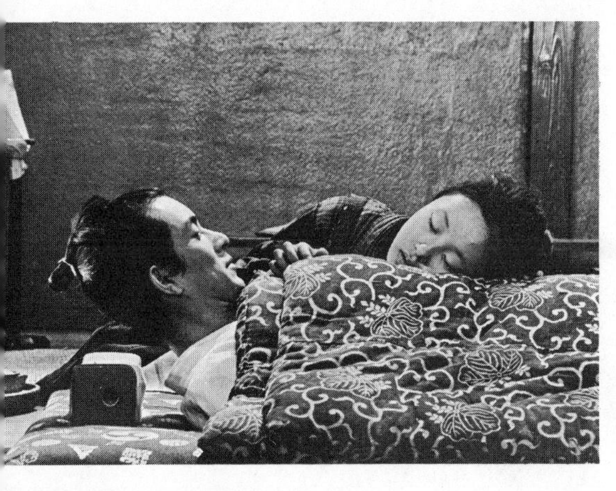

Red Beard, 1965. Directed by Akira Kurosawa. Yuzo Kayama, Terumi Niki.

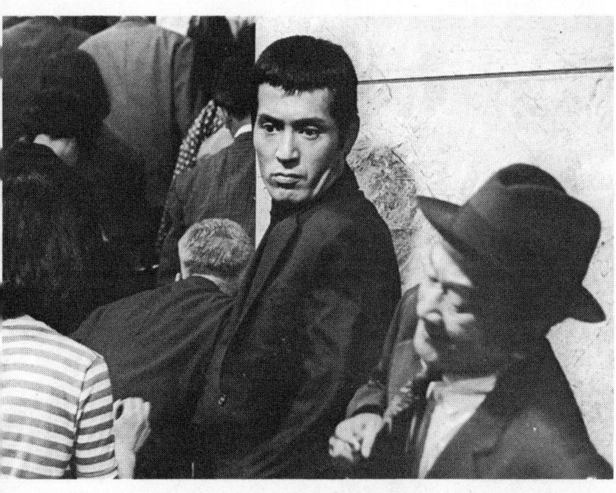

The Age of Assassins, 1966. Directed by Kihachi Okamoto. Tatsuya Nakadai.

The Pornographer, 1966. Directed by Shohei Imamura. Shoichi Ozawa.

Punishment Island, 1966 Directed by Masahiro Shinoda. Shima Iwashita.

Bride of the Andes, 1966 Directed by Susumu Hani Sachiko Hidari (center).

Samurai Rebellion, 1967. Directed by Masaki Kobayashi. Yoko Tsukasa (left foreground).

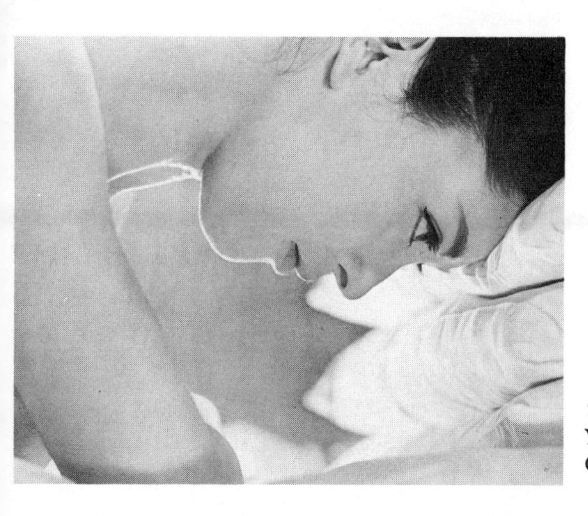

The Affair, 1967. Directed by Yoshishige Yoshida. Mariko Okada.

A Man Vanishes, 1967. Directed by Shohei Imamura.

The Origin of Sex, 1967. Directed by Kaneto Shindo. Nobuko Otowa, Taiji Tamura.

The Inferno of First Love, 1968. Directed by Susumu Hani. Akio Takahashi, Kuniko Ishii.

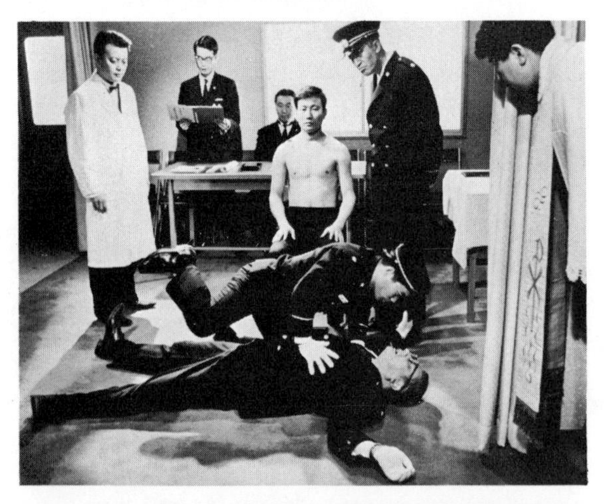

Death by Hanging, 1968. Directed by Nagisa Oshima. Mutsuhiro Tora, Masao Matsuda, Hosei Komatsu, Yundo Yun, Masao Adachi, Fumio Watanabe, Kei Sato, Toshiro Ishido.

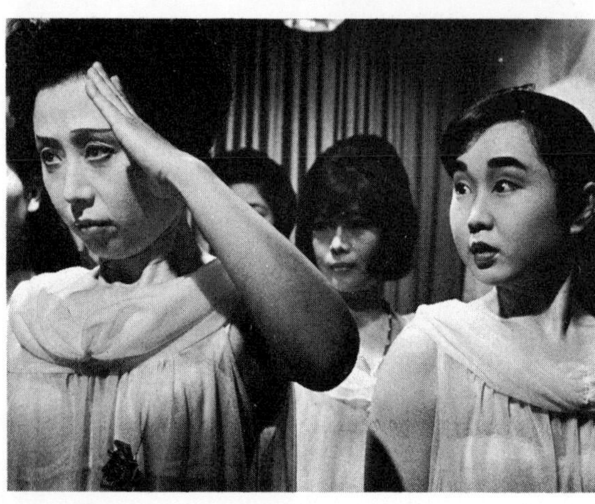

Operation Negligée, 1968. Directed by Kaneto Shindo. Nobuko Otowa (left).

Double Suicide, 1969. Directed by Masahiro Shinoda. Kichiemon Nakamura.

Boy, 1969. Directed by Nagisa Oshima. Tsuyoshi Kinoshita, Tetsu Abe.

Evil Spirits of Japan, 1970. Directed by Kazuo Kuroki. Kei Sato (both figures).

Dodes'ka-den, 1970. Directed by Akira Kurosawa. Yoshikata Zushi.

The Scandalous Adventures of Buraikan, 1970. Directed by Masahiro Shinoda. Tatsuya Nakadai, Shima Iwashita.

The Man Who Left His Will on Film, 1970. Directed by Nagisa Oshima.

stood. Here the Japanese press, confusing freedom with license, is particularly ridiculed. In *Quiet Duel* (Shizukanaru Ketto, 1949), the introspective hero carries the germs of his own dissolution around with him. A young doctor, again played by Mifune, is accidentally infected with syphilis (a "social" disease), knowledge of which is just as destructive as any idea of original sin.

An early but major statement of a similar theme (a lack of compassion rendering an individual's strugglings heroic) is found in *No Regrets for Our Youth* (Waga Seishun ni Kuinashi, 1946). The ruthlessly militaristic prewar government is responsible for the death of a dissident journalist (Susumu Fujita). His wife (Setsuko Hara) determines to be faithful to his ideals. This gentle, cultured Kyoto girl goes to live with his peasant parents. Through a life of hardship and humiliation she finds the will and the strength to continue. She will prevail, will continue to do what she thinks is right.

Kurosawa's continual concern for the individual and this compassionless world in which he lives is shown in a later film, *Dodes'ka-den* (Dodsukaden, 1970), the director's first color film, about the lives of the various individuals in a shantytown. Here Kurosawa returns, twenty years later, to the world of *Drunken Angel*, a junk-filled landscape peopled with those who manage, somehow, to survive. There is a beggar and his little son, a catatonic ragpicker, a couple of laborers and their wives, and a good man with a loose wife. There is no plot, as such, just a recounting of the human misery of the place, redeemed by one man, an old metalworker, who somehow has the strength and the patience to do good.

Kurosawa's most outspoken demand for compassion, however, is *Red Beard* (Akahige, 1965), a very long film, set in the early years of the nineteenth century, about a gruff but humanitarian doctor (Mifune in a role much like that of Shimura in *Drunken Angel*) who, little by little, teaches the meaning of compassion to his young assistant (Yuzo Kaiyama, excellent in one of his few serious roles). Again, as in *The Lower Depths,* good is surrounded by various kinds of misery, and heroism is defined as the ability to continue to do good in the face of indifference, antagonism, and death itself.

Obviously, Kurosawa feels deeply the necessity for human understanding and love. Just as obviously, however, one cannot demand these qualities. The many people who found *Red Beard* sentimental were reacting against an extraordinary demand. Yet the fact that Kurosawa feels free to make such a demand, while it may create art, indicates, at least, the depth of his own feelings and the strength of his own resolution. Films such as *Ikiru,* which show rather than state, are infinitely more persuasive, yet the motivation behind them is the same as that behind *Red Beard.*

Both the feeling and the demand it generates is all Kurosawa's but one is, at the same time, continually reminded of Dostoevsky. Feeling as deeply as he does, it is, then, perhaps, not surprising that his single adaptation from his favorite author should have been a film of very mixed virtues. *The Idiot* (Hakuchi, 1951), a copy of the novel, was conspicuously lacking in the spirit of the original. One cannot, however, justly evaluate this film, since it has never been seen complete. It originally ran over four hours and was released only in a two-hour version. Yet, enough remains to indicate that here again Kurosawa did not realize that merely stating intentions is not enough. The picture is not fully dramatized. Since little is shown, little is consequently believed by any audience.

At the same time, even Kurosawa's comparative failures are the result of his caring too much rather than too little—a rare failing in a film director. Consequently, it is when he moves somewhat away from a direct expression of the compassion theme in his films, when he both views and shows obliquely, through a concern less easily evident, that he, quite naturally, makes his finer films.

For Kurosawa, one of the most fruitful of these oblique angles is his interest in reflecting and interpreting the social world in which he lives. This aim is, of course, an interest quite taken for granted in other countries but in Japan it is not the average director who takes advantage of social issues. Kurosawa, Imai, Horikawa, Kobayashi, Oshima—directors alike only in their interest in controversial social issues—are exceptions to a general rule of Japanese filmmaking. All of the films of Kurosawa mentioned above, for example, are social comments, though it happens that their basic theme is the more important.

Kurosawa's interest in the most pressing—and hence the most controversial—of social issues is seen in films such as *The Bad Sleep Well* (Warui Yatsu Hodo Yoku Nemuru, 1960—a title which might also be translated as *The Worse You Are the Better You Sleep*), a picture whose ostensible theme is the corruption of big business and whose underlying assumption is that absolute power absolutely corrupts.

The picture opens with a very brilliant sequence: an enormous traditional wedding reception in which the hero (Toshiro Mifune) is shown celebrating his marriage to the company president's daughter (Kyoko Kagawa), whom Kurosawa has made lame for much the same reasons that Shakespeare made Ophelia mad. Meanwhile the president himself, beautifully played by Masayuki Mori, amid his unctuous employees, his utterly corrupt board of directors, the full paraphernalia of traditional Japan's most telling ritual, quietly prides himself upon the hope that his line will continue. Into this scene a second wedding cake is brought. It is an enormous and even frightening replica of a downtown office building, into an upper window of which is thrust a single red rose, indicating from where some years before, during a bribery scandal, one of the company officials was pushed. All of this is commented upon by the reporters who are kept waiting outside, and who act as a chorus.

This brilliant sequence sets the tone for the entire film, which is a very strange and very engaging combination of almost Elizabethan concern for power politics (the main plot resembles that of *Hamlet*), completely devastating criticism of a traditional society which even encourages corruption in high places, and pure melodrama. It transpires that the bridegroom is really the illegitimate son of the murdered company official and that revenge is his motivation. He will stop at nothing; he even rescues one of the corrupt officials whom the others think they have murdered in order to introduce him as a "ghost." In one devastating sequence he lets the man witness his own funeral, at the same time playing back tape recordings the others had unwittingly made while making plans for his murder. In the end, however, it is a single virtue that condemns the vengeful hero. He feels sorry for his uncomprehending wife and agrees finally to consummate their marriage. Through her, the father learns of his plans and has him killed. The final scene shows the father on the telephone telling those even higher than himself that the matter has been taken care of—an implication that public corruption goes on and on.

Kurosawa certainly gives his audience no easy way out. *Record of a Living Being* (Ikimono no Kiroku, 1955), also known as *I Live in Fear*, is about a man openly obsessed by the secret obsession of this century —the fear of atomic warfare, of extinction. A successful factory-owner, Toshiro Mifune, is so concerned that he tries to get his family to move with him to Brazil, in the wilds of which he believes he will find safety. The family, complacent and cynical, is outraged by this and tries to have him judged insane. They are right, in that he eventually breaks, and the last we see of him he is in an asylum, looking at the sun and believing that the earth is at last on fire. At the same time there is more than a suspicion that the family is responsible for the father's insanity, that it is their disregard that unhinged him. He is driven to destroy his own factory, which is what they really want, in order that they will escape with him, and it is this fact, more than any other, that puts him into the asylum. Again, naturally, traditional society —in the form of the family—is ultimately responsible.

Kurosawa's classic statement, however, is found in *Ikiru* (1952), a film about the largest possible social issue, and one in which the compassion is found in the way in which the director treats it. A petty official (Takashi Shimura) learns that he is dying. For the first time in his life he realizes that he has accomplished nothing, has never enjoyed anything. He spends the money he has saved in a wild spree but this brings him no satisfaction. Finally he returns to the office and uses all of his strength to bring to realization a petition which has been months on his desk and the desks of others—a request for a park. In the teeth of official disinterest and even antagonism he pushes his project through. Finally it is complete, and that night, sitting on a swing in the park, the snow falling about him, he dies.

Despite Kurosawa's criticisms—and the film, in part, is as sweeping an indictment of bureaucracy as has ever been filmed—*Ikiru* is not an angry motion picture. We are not concerned with a bad society so much as we are with a good man, and Kurosawa makes us realize this by framing the last half of the film with the wake and funeral sequence. The tone is frankly elegiac but there is little *mono no aware*. Instead there is the statement that we are what we do. All the others may be in a state of advanced self-delusion, but the dead man has escaped. He came to know himself and to face his fate.

This honesty animates all of Kurosawa's films but is seen at its best, in high relief, as it were, in his period films, those pictures, which, like the *jidai-geki* of Yamanaka and Mizoguchi, see the past in terms of the present, making their problems and solutions ours, and in so doing rendering themselves timeless.

The simplest and most representative of these films is *The Men Who Tread on the Tiger's Tail* (Tora no O o Fumu Otokotachi, 1945—released in 1952), an hour-long version of the Kabuki *Kanjincho*. It is the twelfth century and a young lord is fleeing the vengeance of his brother. With him, among the other retainers, is the loyal Benkei. They are stopped at a mountain barrier and the lord must impersonate a porter in order to pass. He is suspected, and to avert capture the loyal Benkei brings himself to beat his lord—an act unheard of in feudal Japan. Though the authorities continue to suspect the true identity of the porter they are so impressed by Benkei's selfless action that they allow the party to pass.

This is the plot of the Kabuki and Kurosawa presents it with complete fidelity. His interpretation consists of a single addition—he adds one more porter, a comic figure, extremely well played by the late comedian, Enoken (Kenichi Enomoto)—but one which turns this most traditional of Japanese plays into a most amusing allegory of the modern Japanese man. The porter, completely contemporary, cannot understand the sublimity of any of the actions; he continually gets in the way. More than once he almost ruins everything. He makes mistake after mistake. He alone shows fear—he alone shows relief. And the result is not that feudal standards are criticized but that they are humanized. Few film figures are as human as is Enoken in this picture.

Heroism, dignity, virtue, even bravery for its own sake do not interest Kurosawa; in this he is further from the ordinary period film than was Mizoguchi. Even a film which purposely uses the very stuff of the ordinary *jidai-geki, Three Bad Men in a Hidden Fortress* (Kakushitoride no San-Akunin, 1959), also known as *The Hidden Fortress,* an admittedly heroic story of persecution and flight, is not done in the heroic manner. One of the points is that the three heroes of the title—and this includes General Mifune—are *bad* men.

This is seen even more clearly in *Yojimbo* (1961) and its sequel, *Sanjuro* (Tsubaki Sanjuro, 1962). In both films, the hero (Mifune) is not in himself heroic. In the former picture he pits the two opposing factions of a town (both bad) together and then sits back and watches the fun. In the latter, he is continually harassed by a group of young samurai who really believe in the supposed heroics of their profession. His concern is lest their own foolhardiness kill them.

Kurosawa, unlike many other film directors, is simply not interested in the idealistic, much preferring—flawed though it may be—the human. This is one of the reasons that he likes Dostoevsky. For the same reason he also likes Gorky and Shakespeare, and it is to this that we owe two of his finest films.

The Lower Depths (Donzoko, 1957) is an apparently literal film version of the Gorky play; though the time is the eighteenth century and the place, Edo, now Tokyo. But Kurosawa has illuminated this rather disagreeable drama with a visual magnificence and a really unexpected beauty that makes one quite forget that the original was a play. Not a trace of the stage is left—it is all pure cinema.

The film—like all of Kurosawa's best films—has a very definite and completely individual style. A consistent set of rules governs characters, camera movement, formal composition, and editing. These rules all unify the film, making it a bit more consistent than life itself, and gives that higher realism which we usually call art. Particularly interesting were the new interpretations: the Baron was presented as a real Japanese *tonosama,* a completely lordly lord; the harlot was shown as utterly hysterical; and Luka, the old pilgrim—played by Bokuzen Hidari—became a figure of fun, but at the same time he is the only one who knows what life is about.

The Castle of the Spider's Web (Kumonosu-Jo, 1957), also known as *The Throne of Blood,* was another adaptation, one might almost say an illumination, of a well-known story: that of Shakespeare's *Macbeth.* In transplanting Shakespeare to the Middle Ages of Japan, Kurosawa did little to change the original. Though the characters all had Japanese names, and though the locale was obviously Japan, the story of vaulting ambition and deep desire is both timeless and international in its appeal and it is this quality which Kurosawa both preserved and amplified.

Kurosawa saw in the picture a continuation of a major theme: "I keep saying the same thing in different ways: if I look at the pictures I've made, I think they say, 'Why is it that human beings aren't happy?' Both *Ikiru* and *Record of a Living Being* are such pictures—*The Throne of Blood* on the other hand shows why they must be unhappy." The reasons are the most elemental rules of the human comedy—Kurosawa and Shakespeare both agree on just what they are. So, in this film Kurosawa continued his thesis that power invariably corrupts. Since the story was a legend and the theme timeless, however, he discarded the extreme realism of other historical films, and created a film style which so completely suited the plot that form and content became visually one.

Using only a handful of components—drifting fog and smoke, rainy forests, the shining surface of armor, the sheen of natural wood, the translucence of cloudy skies, the dead white of human skin—Kurosawa, with his cameraman, Azakazu Nakai, created a film with a definite texture. It was as though you could feel it with the hand. More, it was a nearly perfect fusion of film and sound—and one studded with examples of the director's talent.

Just a few were: a marvelous scene—not in Shakespeare—where hundreds of birds, disturbed by the destruction of their forest, fly into the banquet hall and circle around the distraught hero; the sequence where tiny nocturnal sounds form an ostinato to the murder of Duncan; the appearance of the ghost of Banquo where Kurosawa, disdaining trick photography, used the actor himself, made-up in pure white, lights creating a halo around him; the march of the forest, photographed using slow motion and telescopic lens, the trees swaying like gigantic seaweed as wave after wave descends upon the castle, and the superb climax with Macbeth—beautifully played by Toshiro Mifune—immobilized by arrows, the shafts falling in formation on either side of him, piercing his armor, his body, the final arrow transfixing his neck.

The restrained prodigality of this film is but an indication of the multiple worlds that Kurosawa has created. Equally fitting to its subject was the world of *The Lower Depths,* one in which the poverty of the characters was perfectly matched by a photographic finish, which was the precise opposite of the luxurious patina of the *Macbeth* film. It is carefully threadbare, directorial effects being hidden, or appearing only in negative form. The only method of punctuation Kurosawa allowed himself was the simple cut. He confined himself and his actors to just two main sets. He allowed his film no stars as such. There was little music, its substitute being the rhythmic sound of the *hyoshigi,* the clappers which call the audience's attention at the beginning of the traditional theater. These limitations were combined in the brilliant final scene: after the death of the prostitute, the cynic takes a drink, turns to the camera and says: "What a shame! Just when the party was beginning." At the same time there is a single clap from the *hyoshigi* and instantly the end title glows for a second, then disappears, wresting, almost jerking us away from what is indeed a floating world, but one which is also ours.

Just as different was the double world that Kurosawa created for *Ikiru* and *Record of a Living Being*—two films which share a common milieu, one which is seen in *Drunken Angel* and *Stray Dog*, as well as the slight but charming *Wonderful Sunday* (Subarashiki Nichiyobi, 1947), but now the ruins have been rebuilt, sumps have been drained, all is prosperity again. The ruin, the devastation, is in the hearts of men.

In order to emphasize this, Kurosawa in these two films, this double story of two men realizing themselves, one in death, the other in madness, used the most flamboyant, the most prodigal, the most attention getting of styles. The restraint of *The Lower Depths* and of *Rashomon* is completely missing. Here Kurosawa shouts for attention.

Record of a Living Being, wonderfully photographed by Azakazu Nakai, as was *Ikiru*, showed us a disordered world. The camera, like the hero, peers myopically at objects such as telephones and typewriters and they become huge and menacing. The family is habitually seen as a unit, perfectly composed, the staring wide-angle lens holding every member. There is always a distracting element, catching and irritating the eye, as in the scene where the distraught hero goes to visit his young mistress—the jets fly constantly overhead, obscuring the dialogue; an electric fan blows the pages of a magazine at the lower corner of the picture frame; and all of this incessant and meaningless motion confuses and fatigues the eye.

Ikiru presents the same disordered environment, but intensifies it. The film is long and varied; it winds and unwinds; it shifts from mood to mood, from present to past, from silence to a deafening roar—all in the most unabashed and absorbing fashion. One can compare it only to *Citizen Kane,* a film Japan did not see until its 1961 television showings, in which, for much the same reason, the resources of the camera are strained to the limit: the marvelous "night town" sequences in which camera motion is consummately used to suggest the teeming city; the scenes in the office, so hushed and underplayed that they all but shout for attention; the final funeral sequence (the last third of the film) where the life of the dead official is reviewed over and over again, each repetition getting a bit nearer the truth.

In all of Kurosawa's best films the style fits the story so closely that the resulting emotional experience is literally unforgettable. This is seen even in his debut film, *Sanshiro Sugata,* and in its 1945 sequel, where the judo story was reflected in athletic cutting, and in the bounce and pace of the tempo. It is seen fully matured in two of the director's very finest pictures: *Rashomon* and *Seven Samurai.*

The former is extremely well known, probably the most famous Japanese film ever made. Its theme, like that of *Ikiru,* is basically existential: a man is what he does, not what he intends nor what he believes; truth is just as relative as anything else and reality is a matter of interpretation. Kurosawa, who certainly does not consider himself an existentialist, based the film on two stories of Ryunosuke Akutagawa, and was assisted by Shinobu Hashimoto, whose first produced scenario this was. The script as it originally stood—the work of three individuals standing outside and even against the traditional Japanese current—questioned all values.

A lord, his bride, and a bandit meet in a wood. The result is the death of the lord and the probable violation of the bride. There was one other witness, a woodcutter who claims to have witnessed the entire incident, and who compares the various conflicting versions with a servant and a monk, both of whom, like himself, are sheltering themselves from the rain under the great ruined gate which gives the film its name.

It is said that the bandit claims he tied up the lord, violated his bride before his eyes, then killed the husband in the course of a duel; that the wife said the bandit attacked her, then ran away, that the husband hated her for this, that she fainted, and when she revived the knife was in his breast; the dead lord, speaking through a medium—an occurrence related by the priest—said that the violation gave the woman much pleasure and that she tried to make the bandit kill her husband. When both had gone the husband killed himself. Then the woodcutter admits that he actually witnessed the incident. After the attack the bandit said he would marry the woman, that he and the lord should fight for her; the husband, however, refused to risk his life for the sake of such a woman; this infuriated her and it was she who incited them into the duel which killed her husband. All stories are equally plausible, all are probably true—this is what the original script intended to convey, and here it ended.

It was Kurosawa himself who added the epilogue. He has said that the film was otherwise too short and so it probably was. At the same time, however, the addition is so typical of the director that one cannot well imagine the film without it. After the various stories the cry of an infant is heard. The three find an abandoned baby and the servant steals some of its clothing just as the woodcutter had stolen, we find, the woman's dagger. The priest remonstrates, thinking the woodcutter intends to strip the infant, but he merely picks it up, saying that though he has six others at home, one more will not matter. The priest, moved, says: "You have, I think, restored my faith in humanity." This addition is completely typical of the director. It is compassion which, in a way, rights all wrongs; amid a chaos of relative values it is the only absolute.

It is also typical of Kurosawa that he should have chosen for the film the particular style that he did. Of it, he says: "I wanted to return to the simple pictorial values of the silent picture—it is an attempt to bring back the lost beauty of the film." Certainly, so far as pictorial beauty goes, this is a ravishing motion picture. Even Mizoguchi rarely equaled the beauty of the opening scenes, with lord and wife wandering through the forest. The shots of sunlight filtering through foliage may have been inspired by similar scenes in the films of

Dovzhenko and Lang, but they surpass them. The final sequence, with its enormously slow dissolves, each shot farther from the three under the gate, is of the greatest pictorial beauty. The careful composition of each shot, too, is indicative of Kurosawa's concern for the balanced, the beautiful. His placing of three in the forest scenes, a visible and ever-changing triangle, is a visual tour de force. One thinks of other Kurosawa compositions: the controlled diagonals of *The Lower Depths;* the long soliloquy in *The Bad Sleep Well* where Mifune, alone at one side of the screen, is balanced by a rain-flecked window and the diagonal of the half-glimpsed roof beyond; the exciting off-center compositions of *The Throne of Blood;* the father-son scenes in *Ikiru* where the father occupies the bottom half of the screen; the careful asymmetry of the compositions in *Record of a Living Being*. Kurosawa is one of the few directors in the world today who uses pictorial composition to comment upon action.

The acting technique, always interesting in a Kurosawa film, is particularly strong in *Rashomon*. Though foreign critics have found traces of the traditional Japanese theater in the acting, there is little indication that Kurosawa intended this. The *Rashomon* acting style, actually, came from Shingeki and, oddly, from a jungle picture, featuring lions and tigers, which Kurosawa happened to see just before shooting began. He asked his cast—Toshiro Mifune, Machiko Kyo, Masayuki Mori, Takashi Shimura—to attend and take notes. After all, the film was about amorality, one of the strongest animal characteristics. What confused foreign critics was perhaps the grand style which Kurosawa so often uses, personified for most people by the acting of Toshiro Mifune: the grand gestures of Mifune and Isuzu Yamada in the *Macbeth* film; the drunken dances and tantrums of the Gorky picture; the restrained but "big" acting of *Seven Samurai*, larger than anything the West has in either its films, in which acting is habitually the most underplayed element, or in its theater.

In *Rashomon* one also sees the attention to detail which is so typical of the director. When Machiko Kyo drops the dagger in the final version of the story it falls point first into the earth as though into a human breast. The extremely powerful scene where the dead husband speaks through the mouth of the medium appears to be simplicity itself but is actually made up of a vast number of elements, all carefully controlled: the winds, the lightning, the banners in the background, the very sand upon which she kneels. One thinks of telling details in other Kurosawa films: the detailed soundtrack of *The Throne of Blood* with its nocturnal insects, its distant shouts, the constant sound of footsteps; the prodigality of detail, almost a texture, in *The Lower Depths*—rotten cloth, weathered wood, wrinkled skin; the tiny naturalistic actions of the family in *Record of a Living Being*, each one irritating, apparently aimless, ostensibly gratuitous; the pond in *Drunken Angel* upon which float, as though in allegory, the objects of a vanished innocence: lost letters and abandoned dolls.

The fusion of all the elements which make up the completely individual style of Kurosawa occurs in *Seven*

Samurai (Shichinin no Samurai, 1954)—originally shown abroad, before the American remake (1961), as *The Magnificent Seven*—Kurosawa's best film and one which, were it necessary to make the choice, I should call the finest Japanese film ever made.

In a way, it is the summation of everything which is most Japanese about the Japanese film. It is concerned with the present, though its story is laid in the past. It criticizes contemporary values but insists that they are, after all, human values. It faithfully and honestly creates the context of Japanese life, man and his surroundings. At the same time it is concerned with timeless values and universal attitudes. It uses a controlled realism as vehicle and presents a surface of superlative physical beauty which serves to accentuate the beauty beneath.

In many ways *Seven Samurai* is both the opposite and the continuation of *Rashomon*. The earlier film represents the limitations of the intellect: four stories, each completely intellectualized, all mutually incompatible, and all, in their way, "true." *Seven Samurai* on the other hand steps beyond intellectualization. It says that only those acts which spring from emotion are valid acts; that action thus motivated is itself truth. This truth is one which remains, though universally applicable, particularly Japanese. It is one which is shared with Zen and with the haiku, as well as the films of Ozu and Kurosawa—the emotions comprehend where the intellect falters. The basic dichotomy is one recognized and insisted upon in Japan just as much as in the West, and Kurosawa's humanism, his Dostoevsky-like compassion, remains his final and his strongest statement.

In *Seven Samurai*, however, compassion is not sentimentality. It has been tempered with action; theory has become practice. Violent physical action, things done, things accomplished, things completed, things irrevocable: these are what this film is made of. The end result of all this action (and there has rarely been so violent an "action film" as *Seven Samurai*) is the distillation of a single bittersweet and almost unpalatable truth, but one the emotional acceptance of which is impossible to avoid.

The story is simple. A small village, completely defenseless, is harassed by bandits. They ask the aid of a group of masterless samurai, men as homeless, as outside society as the robbers they are asked to fight. They agree, and the body of the film shows their defense, during which a number of them die. The villagers are grateful, but it is spring planting season. They are busy, they have things to do. The remaining samurai leave the town they have defended, the only home they know. They stop in front of the grave of those they left behind, then they move on.

The film is an impassioned call for cooperation among men and, at the same time, suggests why this has always been and will always be impossible. Like *La Grande Illusion*—which it resembles in no other way—*Seven Samurai* demonstrates the essential sympathy binding men together, and shows how war perverts it. But, more, the Kurosawa film goes on to demonstrate that peace too has its perversions. The samurai fight side by side with the villagers; yet, at the end, though the villagers have not become enemies in their turn, at the same time they cannot be called friends. Thus the film constitutes a valid, moving, and unnerving interpretation of the motives of men. That it is not also depressing, even tragic, is due entirely to the sustained conclusion, the scene by the grave, and by Kurosawa's completely atypical but essentially satisfying use of *mono no aware,* that resignation in face of the inevitable which creates the quiet and grave beauty which, in *Seven Samurai,* we recognize as being very close to what we know as catharsis.

Another reason that the tragic statement remains only implicit is that the original script—the work of Kurosawa, Hideo Oguni, and Shinobu Hashimoto—has been realized in terms of visual magnificence. One is so overcome by the splendid animality, by the sheer vitality of the visuals that it is only later that one realizes how near tears one has been. The film is so alive that to remember it is to remember a hundred meaningful images: the opening sword fight in which the swordmaster shows more about the way of the samurai than have all the books ever written about bushido; the funny scene where the head samurai—played by Takashi Shimura—devises a plan to test his men; the character of the last samurai—magnificently acted by Toshiro Mifune—and his death; the love scene in the flowering hills; the first attack of the bandits; their image against the sky, their slow, slow descent through the waving grasses; the last rout and the superb rice-planting sequence, the essence of spring; and the final scene—so profound that its impact is felt only when one realizes how much it is a part of the beginning, how inevitable it is to the whole.

In making the picture—it took over a year to film—Kurosawa created a style the likes of which was never seen in Japan before, or since. For the first time he used superpowered telephoto lenses to capture a feeling of intimacy. The attack of the bandits was thus photographed: men and horses piling up, as it were, to create solid visual images, appearing much closer than they really were. Later Kurosawa made this device a part of his style: the moving forest in the *Macbeth* film; the fight on the mountain top in *The Bad Sleep Well;* the train sequence in *High and Low;* and the fight in *Red Beard.* He also used multiple cameras, each taking the scene from a different angle. Thus he was able to cut directly, without stopping the action, from one perspective to another. The battle in the rain is shot in this manner, and so are the many attacks of the bandits (most of which the West has rarely seen, since this three-and-a-half-hour film was initially shown in most countries with one third of its length missing), as well as the rice-planting sequence. Though this technique uses a vast quantity of film, Kurosawa—who almost invariably shoots at the ratio of ten to one—much prefers it. He used it even in the intimate and much-rehearsed conversation scenes of *The Lower Depths.*

Again, in *Yojimbo,* Kurosawa beautifully fitted technique (including extensive use of telephoto lenses for intimacy, shooting even the most violent of sword fights in this manner) to content, with superb results. The story, which concerns rival gangs in a small town at the end of the Edo period, is composed of the very stuff of the ordinary period film. Toshiro Mifune is the masterless samurai, amused and contemptuous, who sets everything right. But Kurosawa, like Yamanaka before him, infused this common material with new life, returning to even the most notorious clichés their original value. Clichés, film or otherwise, are clichés only because they happen to be true, and in *Yojimbo* Kurosawa's validating of material which the common Japanese cinema had deprived of all life was particularly striking. To take but one example: one of the staple clichés of the period film is a falling fighter's crying *oka* (from *okaasan,* meaning mother) as he dies. Nowadays it is used in a most perfunctory manner, and Kurosawa, seeing it as a challenge, deliberately revitalized it. First in a short scene with a mother and her small son, where it was used with all of the human emotion it retains in ordinary Japanese speech; next in a very funny scene where a weak young man, released by the rival gang, rushes to his mother, and barely gets it out of his mouth before she viciously slaps him; and finally in a fighting scene where a dying gang member gives back to it all the horror and despair and longing for life which rightfully belongs to it.

The very fact that the material is so ordinary makes

one realize, after seeing the film, that Kurosawa has worked a minor miracle, one in which a perfectly controlled style gives new life to even the most hackneyed material. Perhaps one of the reasons is that in *Yojimbo* and *Seven Samurai*, film epics both, one broadly human and comic, the other concerned with idealism and its toll, with the profound capabilities of man, Kurosawa insists upon the intimate. There is a great dependence upon closeups, a constant use of deep focus, low-key photography, and a realistic intricacy of detail which is so compelling, so real, so very believable, that the result is immediacy—it becomes actual.

In Kurosawa, then, realism, the peculiarly Japanese realism, seen in films as early as *Souls on the Road*, reaches its fullest expression. At the same time this realism—which can be compared to the completely different realism of the films of Ozu—is controlled and tempered by style, a style which, though both personal and contemporary, is part of the Japanese aesthetic. Just as in ink-painting, in haiku, or in the woodblock print, the camera, in the hands of a Kurosawa, a Mizoguchi, an Ozu, becomes an instrument of evocation, calling forth the image of the reality of Japan.

In this respect all of the major directors of Japan, no matter how traditional, how individualistic, are alike: they share with the great painters, the great poets, the great printmakers, the great craftsmen of their country, the ability to draw the essence from the world about them, and to present it from an angle of vision, often oblique, which is uniquely theirs, uniquely that of Japan. It is this vision, immaculately honest in the greatest, firmly rooted to a longed-for reality in even the least, which is the aesthetic of Japan—and which has created some of the most beautiful and truthful films ever made.

APPENDIX

Japanese Films Circulated in 16 mm in the United States

Guide to Abbreviations:

AB Audio Film Center and Brandon Films, Inc., affiliated with Crowell, Collier and Macmillan, Inc., 34 MacQuesten Parkway, South, Mount Vernon, N.Y. 10550

CA Cavalcade Pictures, Inc., 959 North Fairfax Avenue, Hollywood, Calif. 90046

CO Contemporary Films, affiliated with McGraw-Hill, Inc., 330 West 42 Street, New York, N.Y. 10036

CV Cinema Ventures, 133 West 14 Street, New York, N.Y. 10012

FI Film Images, a division of Radim Films, Inc., 17 West 60 Street, New York, N.Y. 10023

GR Grove Press, Inc., Film Division, 53 East 11 Street, New York, N.Y. 10003

JA Janus Films, 745 Fifth Avenue, New York, N.Y. 10003

NL New Line Cinema, 121 University Place, New York, N.Y. 10003

NY New Yorker Films, 2409 Broadway, New York, N.Y. 10024

SH Shochiku Films of America, Inc., 4417 West Adams Boulevard, Los Angeles, Calif. 90016

SW Swank Motion Pictures, 2151 Marion Place, Baldwin, N.Y. 11510

UN Universal 16/Universal Education and Visual Arts, 221 Park Avenue, South, New York, N.Y. 10003

WR Walter Reade 16, Walter Reade Organization, Inc., 241 East 34 Street, New York, N.Y. 10016

Yukio Aoshima	*The Bell* (Kane), 1967, 61 min.	AB
Yasuke Chiba	*Downtown* (Shitamachi), 1957, 59 min.	AB
Heinosuke Gosho	*The Neighbor's Wife and Mine* (Madamu to Nyobo), 1931, 64 min.	SH
	The Izu Dancer (Izu no Odoriko), 1935, 94 min.	SH
	Yellow Crow (Behold Thy Son) (Kiiroi Karasu), 1957, 109 min.	SH
Susumu Hani	*Children Who Draw* (E o Kaku Kodomotachi), 1956, 44 min.	AB
	Bad Boys (Furyo Shonen), 1960, 90 min.	AB
	A Full Life (Mitasareta Seikatsu), 1962, 100 min.	NY
	She and He (Kanajo to Kare), 1963, 110 min.	AB

	Bwana Toshi (Buana Toshi no Uta), 1965, 115 min.	AB
	Bride of the Andes (Andes no Hanayome), 1966, 102 min.	FI
Kon Ichikawa	*The Harp of Burma* (Biruma no Tategoto), 1956, 116 min.	AB
	Fires on the Plain (Nobi), 1959, 105 min.	JA
	Tokyo Olympiad, 1965, 93 min. (American Version).	AB
Tadashi Imai	*Muddy Waters* (Nigorie), 1953, 104 min.	AB
	Rice (Kome), 1957, 118 min.	CA
	The Adulteress (Night Drum) (Yoru no Tsuzumi), 1958, 95 min.	SH
Hiroshi Inagaki	*Samurai* (Miyamoto Musashi), 1954, 92 min.	AB
	The Rikisha Man (Muhomatsu no Issho), 1958, 106 min.	UN

Director	Film	Distributor
Keisuke Kinoshita	*The Japanese Army* (Rikugun), 1944, 88 min.	SH
	The Yotsuya Ghost Story (Yotsuya Kaidan), 1949, Part I, 86 min., Part II, 73 min.	SH
	Carmen Comes Home (Karumen Kokyo ni Kaeru), 1951, 75 min.	AB
	The Tragedy of Japan (Nihon no Higeki), 1953, 116 min.	SH
	Twenty-four Eyes (Nijushi no Hitomi), 1954, 155 min.	SH
	The Ballad of Narayama (Narayamabushi-ko), 1958, 97 min.	SH
Teinosuke Kinugasa	*Gate of Hell* (Jigokumon), 1954, 86 min.	SW
Masaki Kobayashi	*Black River* (Kuroi Kawa), 1957, 114 min.	SH
	The Human Condition (Ningen no Joken), Part I, 1958, 212 min., Part II, 1959, 181 min., Part III, 1961, 190 min.	SH

	Harakiri (Seppuku), 1962, 135 min.	SH
	Kwaidan (Kaidan), 1965, 160 min.	WR
Kazuo Kuroki	*Silence Has No Wings* (Tobenai Chimoku), 1967, 106 min.	UN
Akira Kurosawa	*The Men Who Tread on the Tiger's Tail* (Tora no O o Fumu Otokotachi), 1945, 60 min.	AB
	Drunken Angel (Yoidore Tenshi), 1948, 102 min.	AB
	Stray Dog (Nora Inu), 1949, 122 min.	AB
	Scandal (Shubun), 1950, 105 min.	SH
	Rashomon, 1950, 84 min.	JA
	The Idiot (Hakuchi), 1951, the 166 min. version.	NY
	Ikiru, 1952, 140 min.	AB
	Seven Samurai (Shichinin no Samurai), 1954, 141 min. version.	AB
	I Live in Fear (Record of a Living Being) (Ikimono no Kiroku), 1955, 105 min.	AB

	The Throne of Blood (The Castle of the Spider's Web) (Kumonosu-Jo), 1957, 105 min.	AB
	The Lower Depths (Donzoko), 1957, 125 min.	AB
	The Hidden Fortress (Three Bad Men in a Hidden Fortress) (Kakushitoride no San-Akunin), 1958, 126 min.	FI
	The Bad Sleep Well (Warui Yatsu Hodo Yoku Nemuru), 1960, 135 min.	AB
	Yojimbo, 1961, 110 min.	AB/JA
	High and Low (Tengoku to Jigoku), 1963, 143 min.	WR
	Red Beard (Akahige), 1965, 185 min.	AB
Yasuzo Masumura	*The Hoodlum Soldier* (Heitai Yakuza), 1965, 103 min.	AB
Yukio Mishima	*Rite of Love and Death* (Yukoku), 1965, 21 min.	GR

Kenji Mizoguchi	*Sisters of the Gion* (Gion Shimai), 1935, 95 min.	SH
	Utamaro and His Five Women (Utamaro o Meguru Gonin no Onna), 1946, 95 min.	NY
	Women of the Night (Yoru no Onnatachi), 1948, 75 min.	AB
	The Life of Oharu (The Life of a Woman by Saikaku) (Saikaku Ichidai Onna), 1952, 148 min.	NY
	Ugetsu (Ugetsu Monogatari), 1953, 96 min.	JA
	A Story from Chikamatsu (Chikamatsu Monogatari), 1954, 100 min.	NL
	Sansho the Bailiff (Sansho Dayu), 1954, 125 min.	AB
	The Princess Yang Kwei Fei (Yokihi), 1955, ca. 120 min.	CV
	New Tales of the Taira Clan (Shin Heike Monogatari), 1955, 120 min.	NL
	Street of Shame (Red-Light District) (Akasen Chitai), 1956, 85 min.	AB

Noboru Nakamura	*Twin Sisters of Kyoto* (Koto), 1963, 105 min.	SH
	The Three Faces of Love (Sekishun), 1967, 91 min.	SH
	Portrait of Chieko (Chieko-sho), 1967, 125 min.	SH
Yoshitaro Nomura	*Tokyo Bay* (Tokyo Wan), 1963, 83 min.	SH
	The Scarlet Camellia (Akai Tsubaki), 1964, 117 min.	SH
Nagisa Oshima	*Death by Hanging* (Koshikei), 1968, 117 min.	GR
	Dairy of a Shinjuku Burglar (Shinjuku Dorobo Nikki), 1968, 94 min.	GR
	Boy (Shonen), 1969, 97 min.	GR
Yasujiro Ozu	*I Was Born, But . . .* (Umarete wa Mita Keredo), 1932, 89 min.	AB
	The Story of Floating Weeds (The Duckweed Story) (Ukigusa Monogatari), 1934, 89 min.	SH
	The Only Son (Hitori Musuko), 1936, 87 min.	SH

	The Toda Brother and His Sisters (The Toda Family) (Toda-ke no Kyodai), 1941, 105 min.	SH
	Late Spring (Banshun), 1949, 120 min.	NY
	Tokyo Story (Tokyo Monogatari), 1953, 135 min.	NY
	Equinox Flower (Higanbana), 1958, 118 min.	SH
	Floating Weeds (Ukigusa), 1959, 128 min.	AB
	Good Morning (Ohayo), 1959, 93 min.	AB
	The End of Summer (Kohaiyagawa-ke no Aki), 1961, 103 min.	NY
Minoru Shibuya	*The Moderns* (Gendaijin), 1952, 112 min.	SH
Hiroshi Shimizu	*Children in the Wind* (Kaze no Naka no Kodomotachi), 1937, 91 min.	SH
Kaneto Shindo	*The Island* (Hadaka no Shima), 1960, 96 min.	AB
	Onibaba, 1963, 105 min.	CA

Masahiro Shinoda	*With Beauty and Sorrow* (Utsukushisha to Kanashimi to), 1965, 104 min.	SH
	Punishment Island (Shokei no Shima), 1966, 87 min.	AB
Senkichi Taniguchi	*The Sound of Waves* (Shiosai), 1954, 95 min.	FI
Hiroshi Teshigahara	*The Adolescents* (Hatsukoi), 1964, omnibus, 110 min. in all.	CO
	Woman in the Dunes (Suna no Onna), 1964, 123 min.	CO
Toshie Tokieda	*Report from China* (Yoake no Kuni), 1967, ca. 90 min.	FI
Shiro Toyoda	*The Mistress* (Wild Geese) (Gan), 1953, 106 min.	AB
	A Cat, Shozo, and Two Women (Neko to Shozo to Futari no Onna), 1956, 106 min.	AB
	Snow Country (Yukiguni), 1957, 133 min.	FI

INDEX

Dostoevsky, Feodor, 199 ff, 216